"God has entrusted Jonathan Wilson-Hartgrove with a message—the gospel of Jesus Christ has been tragically defaced by American white supremacy and must be reconstructed. In this passionate, fast-paced book, Jonathan gives us a distinctively Christological, hopeful path toward faithful reconstruction. God is able! Even though we, in our structures of sin, often feel powerless to exorcise the demon of white racism, know that God's will shall be done, and God's reign will come because God's purposes shall not be defeated. What an empowering, hopeful word Jonathan has for Christians, white and black."

Will Willimon, author of *Who Lynched Willie Earle?* and *Preaching to Confront Racism*

"In this insightful, accessible volume readers are introduced to the original sin of racism in the United States, which was first and foremost an economic system to benefit the few at the expense of the many. Racism is woven into the fabric of American institutions, and it will require systemic change to bring about true reconciliation. 'A gospel that doesn't confront racism is no gospel at all,' writes Wilson-Hartgrove, for the work of the gospel is to heal that which is divided and to reconcile that which has been torn apart. This book is a must-read for the church."

Elaine A. Heath, professor of missional and pastoral theology, Duke Divinity School

"This powerful and prophetic book should come with a warning label. It's full of stories of ordinary folks working for racial justice, making you want to pull up a chair on the porch for a closer listen. But the stories pack a wallop of conviction, and you will not leave that porch unchanged."

Jana Riess, author of *Flunking Sainthood* and coauthor of *The Prayer Wheel*

"It has become obvious to any who seriously study our sources that much of what we call Christianity in the West today is in radical discontinuity with our faith in its early centuries. Our spiritual healing now depends on corporately facing our past with hope, just as any individual must do in our personal journey to wholeness. Jonathan Wilson-Hartgrove is an honest, courageous, and compelling guide on this path of radical conversion."

Richard Rohr, Center for Action and Contemplation, Albuquerque, New Mexico

"This book offers a front row seat to Jonathan's transformation out of a well-meaning religion marred by white supremacy to a faith that keeps him in the frontlines of the fight for racial justice. His journey will be an inspiration and a roadmap to Christians who desire to be faithful in our times."

Tony T. R. Lin, managing director, Institute for Advanced Studies in Culture, University of Virginia

"For anyone who cares about true biblical justice and is not afraid to ask difficult questions, Jonathan Wilson-Hargrove's masterfully written reflections on his journey of being challenged and mentored by black Christians in America is essential. *Reconstructing the Gospel* shows that such a journey can help us better learn what the gospel really means and why, without it, we are at risk of continuing to perpetuate insufficient justice pursuits informed by a flawed or incomplete gospel. This is a must-read for anyone looking for a more robust, nuanced, and mature faith in the face of America's complicated ongoing history of race and religion."

Ken Wytsma, author of *Pursuing Justice* and *The Myth of Equality*

"The Bible is full of stories of God healing blindness. *Reconstructing the Gospel* is about how God heals a common form of blindness today—racial blindness. You may have it and not even know it, which is why you need this book. By helping you see life in full color, it can help you be saved from the shriveled-heart syndrome and set free from slaveholder religion and the religion of whiteness. This is a beautiful and challenging book for these times."

Brian D. McLaren, author of *The Great Spiritual Migration*

"Racism in American religion, especially in its most subtle forms, isn't something we've had language for describing helpfully—until now. This is a masterful work, invaluable for coming to terms with the hidden wounds of racism and the awful lie that Jonathan Wilson-Hartgrove calls, Christianity of the slaveholder. Jonathan is a reflective soul, at home in his own skin, fully aware of the contradictions and struggles in his own heart. This transparency proves to be the perfect gift for the rest of us who have our own soul work to do in helping end whiteness as a religion."

Peter W. Marty, publisher of *The Christian Century*

"Jonathan Wilson-Hartgrove gets it. In the rubble of evangelicalism's white supremacist crisis, *Reconstructing the Gospel* unflinchingly confesses the ways Christians remain captive to slaveholder religion. Resisting paralysis, it charts a path of personal and political hope. Reconstruction is such an apt word to describe the work we all have to do in light of our nation's history."

Daniel José Camacho, contributing opinion writer for the *Guardian US*

RECONSTRUCTING
THE
GOSPEL

Finding Freedom from
SLAVEHOLDER
RELIGION

JONATHAN
WILSON-HARTGROVE

Foreword by **THE REVEREND DR. WILLIAM J. BARBER II**

≋
IVP Books

An imprint of InterVarsity Press
Downers Grove, Illinois

InterVarsity Press
P.O. Box 1400, Downers Grove, IL 60515-1426
ivpress.com
email@ivpress.com

InterVarsity Press® is the book-publishing division of InterVarsity Christian Fellowship/USA®, a movement of students and faculty active on campus at hundreds of universities, colleges, and schools of nursing in the United States of America, and a member movement of the International Fellowship of Evangelical Students. For information about local and regional activities, visit intervarsity.org.

Published in association with the literary agency of Daniel Literary Group, Brentwood, TN.

Cover design: David Fassett
Interior design: Jeanna Wiggins
Images: preacher: photograph by Arthur Rothstein / Library of Congress
    Union chaplain in uniform: photograph by John Chapin Spooner / Library of Congress
    torn paper: © Daniel Cullen / EyeEm / Getty Images
    flag illustration: © tintin75 / iStockphoto / Getty Images

ISBN 978-0-8308-4534-7 (print)
ISBN 978-0-8308-8648-7 (digital)

Printed in the United States of America ∞

Library of Congress Cataloging-in-Publication Data
A catalog record for this book is available from the Library of Congress.

P	22	21	20	19	18	17	16	15	14	13	12	11	10	9	8	7	6	5	4	3	2	1
Y	36	35	34	33	32	31	30	29	28	27	26	25	24	23	22	21	20	19	18			

CONTENTS

FOREWORD

The Reverend Dr. William J. Barber II

★

*S*o-called white evangelicals, who say so much about what
God says so little—and so little about what God says so
much—have dominated public discourse about religion in
America for my entire adult life. They have insisted that faith is
not political, except when it comes to prayer in school, abortion,
homosexuality, and property rights. They have overlooked the
more than 2,500 verses in Scripture that have to do with love,
justice, and care for the poor, and they have tried to make Jesus
an honorary member of the NRA.

What these so-called evangelicals have done is nothing short
of theological malpractice. With pornographic sums of money
from corporate backers, they have hijacked the gospel and used
it to justify what the Bible calls sin.

I'm not surprised when I meet people who tell me they're ag-
nostic. When I was a guest on the talk show of one of America's

most famous atheists, I told Bill Maher that if you're talking about a god who hates the poor, immigrants, and homosexuals, I'm an atheist too. I don't know that god, and I definitely don't believe in him.

But I am an evangelical because, as my grandmama used to say, "I know Jesus for myself." Between my mother and father's family histories, I count more than eight hundred years of preaching Jesus in my lineage.

In his first sermon—not his second or third, but his very *first* sermon—Jesus said,

The Spirit of the Lord is on me,
    because he has anointed me
    to proclaim good news to the poor. (Luke 4:18)

This is normative preaching in the Christian tradition. The "good news" Jesus proclaims is *euangelion* in the Greek—the root of our word *evangelical*. And it is, from the very beginning of his ministry, good news *to the poor*. I don't know a gospel that doesn't challenge the injustice of poverty.

Biblically speaking, to be evangelical is to be concerned about the poor. The Greek word Jesus uses in Luke's Gospel—*ptōchos*—refers to those who have been made poor by unjust systems. To be an evangelical is to be committed to challenging injustice and economic exploitation. It is the very opposite of the message preached by many so-called evangelicals today.

So what happened to Christianity in America? This is the question my brother Jonathan faces head-on in this book. He follows this question to the heart of America's original sin, and he invites all of us to join him there and face another question: Is our God greater than America's racism?

This is a question we must answer, no matter the color of our skin. Slaveholder religion has infected every corner of the church in America—including the black church. We must never forget that there were enslaved people who accepted the theology fed to them on plantations.

The original sin of racism in America began with a deeply flawed and demonic notion that shaped this nation's development. Bad science claimed that black bodies were biologically deficient, then extrapolated a sick sociology that assumed that people of color had to be placed in subordinate positions. Evil economics perpetuated the lie that money and profit are the chief ends of human existence, and these ends justified almost any means. Slaveholder religion blessed all of this with a heretical ontology, asserting that God ordained racism, slavery, and systems of subjugation. The cumulative effect of this lie threatens not only the witness of Christianity in the world but also our existence as creatures on God's good earth.

Because America's self-deception is so closely tied to the incomprehensible power of weapons that can destroy the world a dozen times over, the immorality of slaveholder religion presents a very real threat to our future. As Dr. Martin Luther King Jr. saw clearly in the last years of his life, we face a real choice between chaos and community—we need a moral revolution. If that was true fifty years ago, then we must be clear today: America needs a moral revival to bring about beloved community.

The main obstacle to beloved community continues to be the fear that people in power have used for generations to divide and conquer God's children who are, whatever our differences, all in the same boat. I will confess—I inherited these fears too. When I met Jonathan twenty years ago, I didn't want to work with white evangelicals in rural North Carolina. People who looked and talked like him burned a cross in my uncle's yard when I was still a boy.

We don't erase the memories we each carry in our body when we come to follow Jesus. But the Jesus I know can make the children of slaves and the children of slaveholders into friends who link arms and work together for justice. This is the story of God's movement in every generation. It's also an experience I've known for myself over two decades of friendship with Jonathan.

With a broad coalition of sisters and brothers from many backgrounds, Jonathan and I are working together to build up a Poor People's Campaign for Moral Revival, taking up the unfinished work of the Poor People's Campaign of 1967–1968 spearheaded by Dr. King. In view of the global challenges we all face, we cannot put off the essential work of reconstructing the gospel. God has given us good news to proclaim to the poor. May it stir us to prophetic action.

Part I

SLAVEHOLDER RELIGION

1

CHRISTMAS ON THE PLANTATION

★

In the small Southern city where I live, developers with an optimistic eye toward progress built a twenty-first-century, glass-walled theater across the street from the county jail. When I read about their plans in the newspaper, I laughed. What a lofty vision for the gravel lot where I parked my car when I drove downtown to visit my imprisoned neighbors through Plexiglas.

But the developers knew what they were doing. Half a decade later, the Durham Performing Arts Center (DPAC) is ranked among the top five concert halls in America. Last year, Aretha Franklin sang "Respect" and Disney's *The Lion King* danced the "Circle of Life" in earshot of a high-rise where five hundred people lived on lockdown twenty-three hours a day. I had to pay to park when I went to see a friend.

Which is why, when Sammie invited me and my family to "Christmas at the DPAC," I was intrigued. Having done more than his fair share of time in the high-rise with barred windows that residents ironically refer to as "the White House," Sammie's not the type that usually fills one of the 2,700 seats across Mangum Street. But he is one of the first people who accepted our invitation when, some fifteen years ago, my wife, Leah, and I moved to Durham's Walltown neighborhood and started asking neighbors to join us for dinner. Since then, we've eaten a thousand meals with Sammie. But I still remember our first conversation when he and I realized that we're the same age—that we grew up watching the same cartoons and going through the same programs in North Carolina's public schools. Only I was white, and Sammie was black. Sammie ran the streets with guys who are locked up in the county jail. I went to grad school with people who frequent the DPAC.

"Christmas at the DPAC?" I asked Sammie when he brought it up. "How we gonna afford that?"

"Here's what you ain't gonna believe," Sammie said, his eyes wide with excitement. "It's free!"

A local megachurch, eager to share the good news of the season, had booked the theater and invited all of Durham to celebrate together at five different shows. Sammie and I made a list of who would want to go and figured out how we could squeeze all twelve of us into Sammie's car and our family's minivan. We had a plan: Sammie would secure the tickets for the late afternoon show on Christmas Eve. We'd all go down together, wish our city a very Merry Christmas, then come home and eat hot dogs Carolina-style with homemade coleslaw. Sammie was excited. He made sure the rest of us were too.

After getting our kids ready, picking up Sammie's cousins, and finding a place to park, we finally made it to our seats in the balcony. The lights were down and a drumline was finishing "The Little Drummer Boy" as the scene shifted to two classical violinists on the other side of the stage. I balanced our youngest on my knee and watched his eyebrows rise in the glow of the stage lights as he took it all in.

No wonder Sammie had been so excited. This was a serious production, highlighting great local talent in an exclusive space where, for today at least, all were welcome. It felt like we were sitting on a little bridge between two worlds, linking one side of Roxboro Road with the other.

"Jesus would be into this," I thought to myself.

No, it wasn't "peace on earth and goodwill toward all people." I knew, of course, that these balcony seats would cost $239 each when *Hamilton* came to town, and our friends locked up across the street still wouldn't be able to make bail. But I'm a sucker for any little way we open ourselves to one another when the days grow shorter and, eventually, even the malls close their doors to honor the birth of the Savior of the world. Our evening at the DPAC wasn't a revolution, but it did feel like a little interruption—a moment to consider how, when we're willing to trust a better way, something better is possible. Even here. Even now.

I was starting to think I could skip my reading of O. Henry's "The Gift of the Magi" this year—that I had my Christmas moment to hold on to—a little light to guard and keep me against winter's wind and the dark night of the soul. I was starting to feel a little bit of that affection we call the "Christmas spirit."

Then the curtain dropped, the house lights came up, and a middle-aged white man walked to the edge of the stage with a Bible in his hand. Before introducing himself, this preacher hemmed and hawed about the amazing talent we'd been enjoying and what a hard act it was to follow—how he taught "every now and then" at the church that was sponsoring this event and how it was his job to "say a word or two" about why we'd all gotten together this afternoon.

The kid on my lap must have felt me tensing up. He wriggled down and crawled over to his mom. I kept hoping it wasn't true, but I sensed what was coming. Alvin, a young African American man who'd come with us, knew it too. He stood up from his seat, climbed over a dozen people, and made a beeline for the exit. I wish I'd joined him. But I didn't.

I stayed to hear about how the angels who sang when Jesus was born in Bethlehem were proclaiming the "good news" that Buddha and Muhammad are dead but Jesus is alive. I listened once more to the neat little syllogism in which Jesus is the logical conclusion to a set of propositions that are assumed to be self-evident. I cringed as the earnest man who'd gone to such pains to dress himself in hipster fashion casually smiled his best smile and invited us to celebrate his message that we were all going straight to hell if we didn't align our understanding of the world with his.

Alvin had seen where this was going from the start. When you live in a world that tells you your existence is a problem, you don't have patience for a religion that says the same with a smile. Soul survival demands a good BS-detector for people who've been labeled black, criminal, ungodly, and undeserving.

But if, like me, you've bowed your head backstage at events like this, praying that the preacher would get it right, you live in hope. Stretched between that preacher's best intentions and the way his message weighed on my friends' bodies, I started to realize I wasn't going to be able to enjoy the hot dog supper Sammie and I had been talking about all week. I looked down from my seat in the balcony and felt a little woozy.

As quickly as he'd come, the preacher was gone, the curtain was up, and the multicultural choir was back again to lead us all in a rousing version of "Joy to the World." I noted that the energetic young man who invited us to sing along started addressing us as "church."

"Stand with me, church. Let me hear you put your hands together, church."

Apparently we had all been baptized by the preacher's words. Now we were "church," and our worship leader was sending us out of the DPAC on a mission.

"We've heard some good news here this afternoon, church. And when you hear good news, you have to tell somebody about it. I want you . . . I want you to go out there and *vomit Jesus on someone!*"

I'd already felt like I was going to throw up. I got out of there as quickly as I could.

For several days after this experience at the DPAC, I walked around in a haze, trying to make sense of the great gap between the joy I'd felt before the preacher's message and the nausea that had followed it. I couldn't simply dismiss the whole affair. After all, he was talking about my Jesus.

I am a preacher. The gospel story lives inside me and pulses to get out like fire shut up in my bones. I've heard lots of bad sermons. I've preached bad ones myself. But this one knocked the Christmas spirit right out of me. Even O. Henry's story felt flat on the page.

What was bothering me, I finally realized, was that Jesus, the person I love most, had become a weapon to drive away someone I also love. Not just in some metaphorical sense. Literally. Alvin had fled the DPAC and found another ride home. The Jesus I know has been knitting our lives together for the past fifteen years, but the message that sent Alvin fleeing was offered in the name of Jesus.

I thought about how cerebral and distant the preacher's bridge between God and humanity felt compared to the visceral gap in my experience before and after his little talk. Not unlike the contrast between the DPAC and the county jail that I confronted again upon exiting the building, feeling every bit like I'd stepped off one of those rides at the state fair that spins you in three directions at once. It wasn't that he'd failed to connect. No, he'd touched a nerve—in Alvin and in me, connecting with hundreds of years of history in a way that made good tidings of great joy feel like an assault.

But how, I kept asking myself, had his good news come to sound so bad? Why did a message he sincerely believed to be gospel for all people send Alvin running for safety and leave me feeling like I'd betrayed my friend . . . and myself?

This was about something more than differing interpretations of the gospel. It was about the integrity of the good news itself. I had to face the breach that is real, not only in the human family and in our world but also in the religion that was passed down to me.

The Gospel Torn in Two

A few weeks after our Christmas at the DPAC, I visited Saint Matthew's Episcopal Church, a quaint chapel one town over from Durham in Hillsborough, North Carolina. This place was never a megachurch, but 150 years ago it was the DPAC of its day. North Carolina's elite donated the land and built this chapel in 1824. Their children intermarried, and by the end of the Civil War a member of the church, Paul Cameron, was the wealthiest man in North Carolina. He owned most of the land that is now Durham County and nearly a thousand enslaved human beings.

Saint Matthew's priest showed a small group of us the balcony, which was added to the church mid-nineteenth century to segregate its enslaved members from the landed gentry below. Those Southern gentlemen imagined themselves as great fathers, writing often in their personal letters about "our family, black and white." But they also understood the necessity of distinction. The whole plantation economy rested on every person knowing the difference between slave and free.

We were standing at the front of the chapel, looking up at the balcony in the back, when a fellow visitor turned to the Communion rail behind us and asked, "Were masters and slaves segregated when they came forward for Communion?"

"Oh, no," the priest said matter-of-factly. "They had very good sacramental theology. 'One Lord, one faith, one baptism; one God and Father of all.'"

He recalled an annual report from one of his predecessors who'd gone on to serve as bishop of North Carolina in the mid-nineteenth century. In it, the bishop reported on an Easter service he'd conducted in eastern North Carolina at a plantation that had its own chapel. He waxed eloquent about how preparations had been made to adorn the building and about the exceptional music that was performed. Then he described the scene of master and slave kneeling together at the altar, receiving the body and blood of Christ. It had seemed to him a notable image of the reconciliation that Jesus Christ makes possible.

"But is there any record of an experience like that making someone question slavery itself?" The young white woman who asked the question seemed troubled. I think she was feeling in her gut something like what I'd felt on my way out of the DPAC a few weeks earlier.

The priest paused for a long time to consider her question. He knew his parish well, the living and the dead. This was not the first time he'd considered the gospel's impact on their lives.

"We do know that one freedman left this parish and became an abolitionist in Oberlin, Ohio. I like to think it was because of something he'd seen and heard in this church." The priest could see how desperate this woman was for a word of assurance—for some sign that the gospel has power, not simply to remind us of what should be but to change who we are.

If he'd stopped there, part of me would have been happy. One abolitionist in a thousand is at least a glimmer of hope—even if he did have to flee this space to live out what he heard in the Scriptures. But looking at our little group of visitors, all pale-skinned, the priest knew he had to tell another story—one about someone far more like most of us.

Thomas Ruffin donated the land where Saint Matthew's still sits today. He was an upstanding white citizen of North Carolina in the nineteenth century and a lifelong member of the parish, where the fellowship hall still bears his name. Ruffin was also a justice on North Carolina's Supreme Court. When a white man was convicted of assault against a woman he hired, Ruffin's court voted in the *State v. John Mann* to overturn the white man's conviction. Ruffin wrote the opinion himself.

The priest had read Ruffin's words with a pastor's eye. He could see the man who is still buried in Saint Matthew's graveyard wrestling in every sentence with the reality he experienced at the Communion rail each Sunday. Ruffin went to great lengths to acknowledge the humanity of the slave. But legal precedent was clear. "The power of the master must be absolute," the white churchman wrote, "to render the submission of the slave perfect." Reading Ruffin's opinion, the priest said, was "like watching a man tear himself in two."

I thought about the two worlds that Sammie and I grew up in and the two sides of Roxboro Road—about how fractured our world is and how, deep down, each of us longs to see it made whole. I thought about how the same gospel that made some Christians want to sing praise music had sent a black person running for freedom in the nineteenth century and another fleeing the DPAC in the twenty-first century.

Standing there in Saint Matthew's, I had an epiphany about the gospel, the old, old story whose words I'd known since before I'd begun to grasp their meaning as a powerful force. I've seen it transform lives, lift up the brokenhearted, and spur people from bondage toward freedom. But like every good gift from God, the story of Jesus has been hijacked to serve the opposite of what God wants. The institutions of Christianity, the words of Scripture, the very message of the gospel was twisted 150 years ago to endorse what we now readily confess is sin.

This was not the exception, but the rule. The one sister who heard something different at Saint Matthew's had to flee north, all the way across the Ohio River, where she was still breaking federal law when she greeted formerly enslaved sisters and brothers as fellow children of God, not stolen property.

Christianity in America has not occasionally turned away from the gospel's truth, like a sailor tempted by the sirens' call. It has, rather, turned the gospel against itself, tearing in two the people who adopted this form of religion without letting its truth change their lives. This subversion of the gospel put a crack in the foundation of our common life. It opened up a great gulf between people that has thwarted our pursuit of genuine community ever since. And it has left a hidden wound deep in our hearts. Standing in the sanctuary where Thomas Ruffin worshiped every Sunday, that great passage from the prophet Isaiah rang in my head: "And you shall be called Repairer of the Breach" (Isaiah 58:12 WEB).

Sometime or another, we all sense that things aren't as they should be. It's why the young white woman hoped to discover at the Communion rail some link between the slave balcony and the master's pew. It's why I'd longed to experience a hint of reconciliation at a Christmas celebration where all of Durham could sit down together and sing carols without throwing up on anyone. I guess it's even what the preacher was trying to build with his bridge between God and humanity that couldn't begin to comprehend the gulf between him and Alvin.

But the religious experience of a slaveholder compelled me to confess that I'd been as blind as that zealous evangelist, as naive as the young woman who'd hoped against hope that her theology trumped history. I'd deceived myself into thinking that the original sin that ripped this nation in two had somehow not formed me. In a chapel built by plantation owners nearly two centuries ago, a priest told me the truth: *I am a man torn in two.*

I don't just live in a divided world. *I* am divided. And if it's true all the way down—not just for me, but for the sisters and brothers who've loved and taught me, then I must confess this also: *the gospel I inherited is divided.*

I know this might not sound like good news, but I received it like a man who's been sick for a very long time, dealing with symptom after symptom, finally getting a diagnosis. My soul cannot be well without the society that made it sick finding health.

But that is not all. The gospel that was twisted to accommodate America's original sin must also be reconstructed if we are to experience the healing that Jesus wants to bring. Otherwise, evangelism is violence and those of us who spend our time in church meetings are perpetuating a death-dealing culture without even realizing it.

Spiritual Reconstruction

Another way of saying this is, Christians in America must come to terms with how *institutional racism* has infected us. Few white persons in twenty-first-century America see themselves as racist. (Even fewer Asian, Latino, or African American persons do.) Most American Christians—white, black, or brown—are horrified by the idea of a Ku Klux Klan (KKK) rally or by the public personality who occasionally gets caught saying the n-word. But personal animus against others because of the color of their skin isn't the racism that turned the gospel against itself. Remember, enslaved people were "family" to Paul Cameron and Thomas Ruffin.

The sin that ripped the gospel in two—the spiritual root of our political divisions and class disparities—is a lie that was told centuries ago to justify owning, using, and abusing other human beings. Racism is about implicit bias as much as it's about public policy. It's why a white applicant with a criminal record is as likely to get a job as an African American with no criminal history. And it's why African American veterans of World War II didn't benefit from the GI Bill—legislation offering educational funding, low-interest housing loans, and other support for veterans—the same way their white counterparts did. It is why, two and three generations later, the median disparity between the wealth of white and black families hasn't changed, despite the advances of the civil rights movement. Racism is why historically black neighborhoods across America are gentrifying at breakneck speed while the families who built and sustained these communities are being displaced.

This is what racism means: we live in a society that continues to be divided, and we are, each and every one of us, split in two ourselves. When white Christians refuse to hear cries for justice from black and brown sisters and brothers, it is one more symptom of the racism that has long divided our souls, our congregations, and our nation. When middle-class Americans silence the voices of poor black and brown people who know from daily experience that race and history still matter, our hardness of heart betrays a spiritual sickness that Jesus detected in the Pharisees of his own day. We, like them, have turned the gift of God's law against itself. Splitting the good news in two, we refashion it as both a shield against God's grace and a sword to wield against our neighbors. We turn God's good news into our bad news.

Fifteen years ago, Leah and I moved to Durham's Walltown community, a historically African American neighborhood whose residents have maintained Duke University since its first janitor, George Wall, moved here in the 1890s. Ignorant of much of Walltown's history, we relocated to a place that has taught us what it means to be white. People like Sammie welcomed us into a community where we've worked and worshiped—where our kids play under the watchful eyes of grandmas who sit on their porches and young men who walk these streets, wondering whether their lives matter to anyone else. One of them knocked on the door not long ago and asked, clearly worried, if I knew my two-year-old was playing alone on the porch. No one needs to tell this young black man that all lives matter.

In this place, neighbors and friends have taught us to see racism—to name the ways history still shapes the present and to doubt the certainties we inherited along with being white. These people, together with the Holy Spirit, have stirred up a passion within me to face America's original sin in my own heart and to join the freedom movement that is committed to exorcising it from our common life. They have shown me how a gospel that doesn't confront racism is no gospel at all. In a moment of clarity—seeing myself and my gospel ripped in two by this shared history—Saint Matthew's helped me to finally name what had left me feeling sick on Christmas Eve.

For all my life I've known that the gospel must reconstruct my life. Whatever humanity's problems, Jesus is the answer. This I believe.

But what do you do when you realize that your Jesus has been ripped in two—that the name of the one who came to set us free has been hijacked by the principalities and powers that bind us? What happens when, like Mary in the garden, you realize they've taken away your Jesus and you don't know where they've laid him?

It is not easy to pray in the midst of such a faith crisis. You find yourself questioning the One you're used to going to with your questions—wondering if you're talking to the true and living God or some projection of your privilege that you fashioned in your own image.

But a good diagnosis at least clarifies the situation. Better to see how you've been deceived—how, even, you've deceived yourself—than to miss the gospel because you thought you already had the answer.

I call it the foggy morning of the soul—that liminal time when you can see just enough to pull the car out of your driveway—but you aren't quite sure you see where you're going. We turn our headlights on in such a situation. We sit on the edge of our seats, eyes wide open to detect whatever might emerge before us. We are afraid, yes. But we lean in, because there's no other way to get where we are going.

This is why Jesus said that the poor are blessed and the hungry will be satisfied and the merciful will be shown mercy. Not because God loves them any more than he loves the rest but because they know their need. They have a clear diagnosis. A hungry man knows he needs bread. A heart that's been broken knows it wants mercy. And a soul that can see its own self-deception knows it needs good news, which is what the gospel is.

A friend of mine calls it the End-of-Your-Rope Club. There are a thousand ways to get there, but however we come to the end of our ropes, it is the place where we discover that our only hope is a love that comes from beyond us. Maybe you've thought you've known the gospel all your life. Maybe you've always thought it sounded like some crazy con. Whatever your background, the only good news that's worth believing comes through loud and clear at the end of your rope. This is where you learn you need a Savior.

After my epiphany at Saint Matthew's, I went back to the texts we call the Gospels. I read again those four accounts of Jesus' life and death, and I saw in a way I'd missed before how the diagnosis of a divided faith is the beginning of the good news Jesus offered to nearly every religious person he met during his time here on earth.

Jesus prayed the psalms and quoted the Torah and spent time in the temple, but his message to religious people was surprisingly grim. "Woe to you . . ." was his constant refrain. When he took a more pastoral tone, it was usually something like, "Don't you remember where it is written . . . ?"

After reading the Bible all my life, I realized that Jesus, who was a preacher, didn't really say anything that hadn't been said before. In fact, he took pains to make clear that he was saying what the God of Israel had been saying ever since God spoke the world into existence. "I have not come to abolish them [the Torah and the Prophets] but to fulfill them" (Matthew 5:17).

Jesus didn't come to preach a new gospel. *Jesus came to reconstruct God's good news, which religious leaders had turned against itself.*

How had I missed this? How have so many sincere Christians confessed and practiced a religion that made them worse than they might have been otherwise? How, I had to ask, did slaveholder religion take a message that calls all of us out of systemic injustice and use it to subjugate generations of children created in the image of God?

Following America's Civil War, the moral contradiction at the core of American history had literally ripped the nation in two. Americans were a people at the end of their rope. Humbled by grief and loss, they sought language to name a shared journey toward a common future. *Reconstruction* was the name they gave their brief attempt to make formerly enslaved people full citizens of the United States. Because that effort was subverted by people who called themselves Christian, slavery did not end. It evolved into Jim Crow in the South, segregated ghettos in the North—an existence both separate and unequal. A Second Reconstruction confronted this fundamental contradiction again in the mid-twentieth century through a nonviolent struggle led by people of deep faith. Though the civil rights movement's stride toward freedom is memorialized on road signs and in a national holiday that bears the name of Reverend Martin Luther King Jr., a Moral Majority emerged in the 1980s to subvert almost every systemic change Dr. King had died for. The Jim Crow laws intended to separate the races evolved to subvert Reconstruction.

This book is a reckoning with my own faith's past and with the many ways Christianity in America remains captive to slaveholder religion. It is a confession, for sure, but I'm not just baring my soul. I've tried to tell the truth about the churches where I work and worship and the nation in which I seek to be a faithful citizen. Ours is a shared story, and all of us bear some responsibility for the mess we are in.

Staring this history down has convinced me that reconstruction is, in fact, what Jesus has always been about. But we can't even see this until we learn to deconstruct much of what we assume is given about ourselves, our churches, and our nation. We have so much to unlearn before we can learn the things that Jesus lived, died, and rose again to teach.

This is an American story but one told with an awareness that the economy that developed on the plantations of the South is now commonly called the "global economy." The moral contradiction, with which I am intimate by accident of birth, now threatens to destroy the entire world. It has taken me decades to learn to see this, and I'm certain I still don't comprehend it. But I ask your patience as I try to peel back the layers of slaveholder religion in the first half of this book.

Please do not lose hope. This book is, as its title claims, about how Jesus can reconstruct the gospel to free us from false religion. This is what the Christianity of Christ has always been about. But the biggest obstacle to reconstructing the gospel in America has been (and continues to be) the compromised and corrupted religion of the slaveholder. For the next five chapters, I'm trying to expose how *racial blindness*, *racial habits*, and *racial politics* are tied together in the slaveholder religion that has been passed down to in America us simply as "Christianity."

God has a way of interrupting us—of laying open the wounds of our past in ways that touch us personally. This, too, is the gospel, which is why each chapter in the first half of this book also demonstrates how tearing down is central to the ministry of Jesus in all four Gospels of the New Testament. Whenever any of us come to the end of our rope, we face a personal crisis. Whenever all of us come to the end of our rope collectively, we face a social crisis. No one chooses the agony of times like these, but Jesus meets us here at the end of our rope.

Still, Jesus does not leave us here. As long as there has been slaveholder religion, there has also been the Christianity of Christ, inviting people and communities into *fusion politics*, *surprising friendships*, and *inner healing*. This, too, is written into our Scripture and history, and such reconstruction is the theme of the second half of this book. I am writing as I hope to preach and live—with a deep sense of calling to help save the soul of America and sound a warning cry to a world on the verge of disaster. Time is short and the stakes are high.

But as broad as the implications of reconstructing the gospel may be, the heart of this book is deeply personal. It is about the songs my parents and grandparents sang to me and the faith I hope to pass on to my children. This book is a love letter to them, and to you. Where it stings, I pray you can trust that its words are hot with the fire of love.

2

IMMORAL
MAJORITY

*E*ight years after the end of the Civil War, on Easter Sunday 1873, the white men of Grant Parish, Louisiana, were conspicuously absent from their families' dinner tables. It is unclear how many of them had attended church that morning, but by noon some three hundred souls were assembled with rifles in hand outside the Colfax Courthouse. Though it might have appeared of little consequence to an outside observer, this courthouse had become a contentious symbol since the election of 1872, both to the black men who armed themselves to defend it and to the white men who abandoned their traditional Easter celebrations that Sunday to violently regain control of local government.

After the Confederacy's surrender, states such as Louisiana, which had been in rebellion against the Union, were placed under federal oversight during Reconstruction. The Colfax Courthouse was a recently converted barn on William Calhoun's plantation, but it was the local seat of government for the area that had been renamed Grant Parish after the Union general who defeated the Confederacy before becoming president of the recently re-United States. Its capitol, which consisted of little more than the renovated barn, was named after Grant's vice president, Schuyler Colfax.

Though they had elected mostly white leadership in 1872, black men armed themselves to defend a local government named after Northern white men because it was the first government for which they had been able to vote. With confidence that Washington would send reinforcements, the formerly enslaved population of Grant Parish held their ground, fending off gunfire well into the afternoon on Easter Sunday.

As the fighting wore on, the white militia pointed its cannon at the courthouse, and about half of the besieged faithful decided God might more easily answer their prayers if they made a run for it. Forty black men were overtaken before they made it to the river. Their captors firebombed the courthouse, forcing them to watch friends they'd left inside flee from flames into gunfire. Then they marched the black men to a nearby cotton field and executed them. It was Easter Sunday 1873, and the South had risen again.

After the Colfax massacre, white paramilitary groups across the border in Mississippi imitated the violence of Grant Parish. An unofficial alliance between the Democratic Party and these Klan-like groups proved successful in suppressing black Republican voters, who were determined to support the party of Lincoln. Known as the Mississippi Plan, this strategy was only successful in ending Reconstruction when the Compromise of

1877 allowed Ohio Republican Rutherford B. Hayes, who had narrowly lost the popular vote, to become president as long as he promised to remove all federal troops from the South. The help that the defenders of the Colfax Courthouse had prayed for on Easter Sunday would not be coming from Washington—not for three quarters of a century at least. Southern legislatures quickly passed Jim Crow laws, and the promise of full citizenship for African Americans faded into the legal fiction of "separate but equal," the doctrine confirmed in the *Plessy v. Ferguson* Supreme Court decision of 1896.

Most Americans do not remember this period following the Civil War as a time that was in fact *more* violent for African Americans in the South than the tumultuous war years. For most of the twentieth century, stories about Reconstruction were shaped by the so-called Dunning School, named after William Archibald Dunning, who taught at the prestigious (and Northern) Columbia University in the early twentieth century. A whole generation of Dunning's students wrote books arguing that Reconstruction failed because its demands were too radical. Carpetbaggers and railroad barons exploited the defeated South for financial gain, they said, leading to a backlash against "immorality" and "corruption." The white men who stood up to defend their native South had called themselves Redeemers, claiming divine blessing for their cause. In their minds, they had not forsaken their Lord when they attacked the Colfax Courthouse on Easter Sunday. They had, instead, christened the violent white supremacy campaign that would overthrow Reconstruction as the Redemption movement.

I grew up in North Carolina's Bible Belt in the 1980s, assuming the spirit of Redemption, even if I didn't know the ugly details of its history. Those were the glory days of another "moral" movement—the Moral Majority—when Ronald Reagan addressed the National Association of Evangelicals saying, "I know this is a non-partisan gathering, and so I know that you can't endorse me, but . . . I endorse you and what you're doing."

At the very least, he counted on our votes. And my people were glad to give them. Never mind that Reagan, an actor who'd arisen from the fleshpots of Hollywood's celebrity culture, had cut his political teeth in California. I remember serious conversations in the community where I grew up about how, due to the widespread depravity of Southern California, God might swallow the whole state into the Pacific Ocean with a single earthquake. Even still, Reagan was our man. He was against abortion. He was against big government. And he was pro-family. Despite the liberal media and Communist-leaning universities, Reagan would save us all.

Bless his heart, he even blinded us to our inherited racism by establishing the Martin Luther King Jr. holiday with that broad and hopeful smile. Sure, slavery and Jim Crow were blemishes on our collective record. But ours was a story of redemption—a forward-looking faith that described mistakes as a failure to live up to our ideals and pledged allegiance to our common belief that we were a chosen nation. The corruption of big government and the disorder of the 1960s counterculture had led us to the brink of national destruction. (Little matter that Dr. King had argued for a *bigger* war on poverty and joined the counterculture to condemn the war in Vietnam before saying that America may, in fact, go to hell.) Remembered as a domesticated preacher who focused on the "content of their character," King became a household demigod of American civil religion, perpetuating the Redeemers' myth in a new, postracial chapter of American history.

As a young Southern Baptist political hopeful, I believed all of this without question. Jesus was a Republican, America was on the right side of history, and I was going to climb the ladder—through humility and service, of course—from small-town North Carolina to Pennsylvania Avenue. All I needed was time and opportunity.

As it happened, Senator Strom Thurmond gave me the foot in the door I was looking for when he invited me at sixteen years old to serve in his Washington, DC, office as a Senate page. The longest-serving member of the US Senate at the time, Thurmond had weathered the political winds of the South, running as a Dixiecrat candidate for president in 1948 and filibustering the 1957 Civil Rights Act, only to cross the Rubicon in 1968 and lead the Dixiecrats into the Republican Party of Nixon and Reagan. I was introduced to Thurmond's social imagination the first time I walked into his office. "Welcome to DC, son," he said with a firm handshake, stepping out from behind his large oak desk and looking me in the eye. His advice was singular: "Look out for yourself. This is a dangerous town."

Dangerous, he seemed to suggest, in the same way Colfax, Louisiana, had been dangerous under "Negro rule." Dangerous in the way America's cities had seemed explosive when, nearly a century later, the disenfranchised black people of the South asserted their right to register as voting citizens and defend themselves against brutal attack. I was to understand in a single word—in the grip of a hand, the nod of a head—that I had been called to participate in the serious business of maintaining law and order over and against a vague but ever-present danger. All of this, I gathered, was my Christian duty.

Then one crisp fall day, as I was walking from Thurmond's Senate office to Union Station, an African American man who was holding a Styrofoam cup asked if I could spare some change. His request was basic enough—one man asking another for help. But I could not see the man. A dividing wall stood in my imagination to protect me from him. In a word, he was dangerous. Not just to me, but to society. "The undeserving poor," we called him. I kept walking.

As I was reaching out to grab the handle of the large glass door at Union Station, I heard the voice of Jesus speak to me in the King James Version I had memorized in Sunday School: "Inasmuch as ye did it not to one of the least of these, ye did it not to me" (Matthew 25:45). The man I'd just ignored wasn't simply asking for money. He was calling me to account. He was Jesus, and he was trying to save me from a religion that was making me worse.

Slaveholder Religion and the Christianity of Christ

American Christians in the Obama years half hoped we'd moved beyond race. Yes, the civil rights movement was a moral cause, we told ourselves. But we have moved beyond that now. We took down the Whites Only signs, integrated the schools, and saw a black man rise to this nation's highest office. "Today's justice issue isn't race, but class," some said. Others were even more dismissive: "African Americans need to stop blaming others and take responsibility for the problems in their communities."

Yet even as President Obama was in office, their communities were gentrified. Young white professionals moved back to urban centers, bringing with them the very American assumption that whoever owns the property owns the neighborhood. When new neighbors were frightened by hoodie-wearing "natives" in New

York, Baltimore, Oakland, and Detroit, these former suburbanites called the cops. Integrated police forces were deputized to defend the property rights of the new colonizers against black and brown neighbors they'd learned to fear by watching shows like *COPS*. And we thought we'd left race behind?

Young people of color who were tired of being stopped, frisked, and shot dead in the only place they'd ever called home found one another on Twitter and united around a hashtag three black women were using to raise a cry for racial justice—#BlackLives Matter. When they occupied their cities' streets after the deaths of Mike Brown, Eric Garner, Tamir Rice, Freddie Gray, and Sandra Bland, they became a movement and connected with veterans of the black-led freedom struggle, who helped them see how their fight was but another link in a long chain. "All lives won't matter until black lives matter," they said. And they invited me and others to join them in this fight for a more perfect union.

Robert, a young man who led the Black Lives Matter movement in Durham, called to ask if I'd help him recruit some kids to see Ava DuVernay's movie *Selma* about the fight for voting rights in Alabama in 1965. We found a hundred young people to view the movie together on opening night. As the credits rolled at the end, Robert stood at the front of the theater and declared, "The same fight they were fighting then, we're fighting now!" He led about forty young people into the hallway, where they lay down for four minutes of silence to memorialize the four hours Michael Brown's body was left lying in the street in Ferguson, Missouri.

A few weeks later, Robert called to tell me he was running for city council. I invited him to make my office his campaign headquarters, and over the next several months I watched middle schoolers who'd joined the "die-in" at the movie theater learn how to work a phone bank to raise money for a campaign and get out the vote. Robert won the primary race, and I saw hope dance in those kids' eyes. When he lost in November, their spirits weren't crushed. "I'm going to put the experience on my résumé," Isaiah, one of the young men, told me. Black Lives Matter had helped him to see that he was somebody in a way that no Bible study or after-school tutor ever had.

How, I asked myself, had I missed it? In all of my genuine concern for these kids who I've known and cared about since they were born, how had I failed to see that the healing and hope Jesus most wants to give them can't be separated from a prophetic truth telling that confronts the systemic injustices they feel weighing on their bodies? What kept me from seeing this gospel?

I thought about the Colfax Courthouse and Strom Thurmond and all the subtle ways I had learned to imagine my Christian duty as a call to subdue the dangerous inner city and redeem America from the problems that we too easily associate with blackness. No, I wasn't a conscious white supremacist. I didn't have Klan robes hidden in my closet. But for far too long something had kept me from seeing the essential connection between a young black man's spiritual growth and the possibility of political power and cultural imagination that Black Lives Matter offers. Even in Obama's America, I was practicing a racially fragmented faith.

And I wasn't by any means alone. During the campaign of 2016, I watched news coverage of a campaign rally in Fayetteville, North Carolina, where thousands gathered to cheer Donald Trump's promise to "Make America Great Again." It was, I noticed during the camera pan, an overwhelmingly white crowd. But there, amid the sea of people, a Black Lives Matter activist stood to object. He didn't hear the hope of better economic times that his white neighbors cheered. He heard old hatred and fear. He heard the ringing endorsements of the KKK, and he knew that Trump's crusade against Obama's citizenship had not been about a birth certificate—it had been about the imagined danger of a black man in the White House.

"Get 'im outta here!" Trump shouted. Security officers cuffed the Black Lives Matter activist's hands before leading him through a jeering crowd. Somewhere in the mayhem, an older white man punched the young black man in the face.

I thought of Robert's "die-in" on the theater's carpet. I thought about those young guys calling from a phone bank to tell people they'd never met about Robert's vision for One Durham. Where Trump and his supporters saw a menace to society, I saw Jesus. The same Jesus who'd breathed hope into kids I love took a beating on national television and was locked up.

Months later, when 81 percent of white evangelicals told exit pollsters that they voted for Donald Trump, I was sad. But I could not be surprised. A son of the South, I inherited a white identity that knew how to worship Jesus on Easter Sunday morning and stamp out "Negro rule" in the afternoon. Our dead are buried among monuments that praise the "Christian virtue" of slaveholders. We sing "Amazing Grace"—that anthem written by a repentant former slave-ship captain—in spaces where grace has been hijacked by a way of life rooted in every one of the seven deadly sins. No, I have no room to judge. I can only confess.

But this confession that my life is entangled in my country's original sin of race-based slavery grows out of a grace—the gift of Black Lives Matter to Isaiah and to me. Karl Barth said we only know sin on our way out. He was echoing Augustine. To confess is also to announce that you've seen something new. It is to name, as best as I know how, how the Jesus of Black Lives Matter is saving me from the Jesus of Colfax Courthouse. More and more I realize that reconstructing the gospel is, first and foremost, about knowing which Jesus we follow.

After Frederick Douglass recounted the horrors of living as chattel and the drama of his fight for freedom in what would become the nineteenth century's most famous description of slavery, the reality of multiple Christs haunting the South emerged as the subject of an appendix to his autobiography. He did not need the epiphany I would experience over a century and a half later in an Episcopal church. He knew from experience that Jesus had been split in two. But he also didn't want to be misunderstood. Douglass knew and trusted Jesus. He wanted a reconstructed gospel to save him and his country.

"I find, since reading over the foregoing Narrative," Douglass wrote, "that I have, in several instances, spoken in such a tone and manner, respecting religion, as may possibly lead those unacquainted with my religious views to suppose me an opponent of all religion." The formerly enslaved Douglass had exposed the hypocrisy of his Christian slavemaster and a Christian society that would defend the master's right to hold people as property. He'd exposed the sin and inhumanity of slavery by simply telling his story.

But Douglass's experience begged a distinction—a point of clarification amid dizzying self-deception. Though he had rebelled against the teachings of the slaveholders' religion (think "Slaves, obey your earthly masters" [Ephesians 6:5]), Douglass found a life-giving message of freedom in the teachings of Jesus. His experience of divine grace taught him the difference between, as he said it, "the Christianity of this land, and the Christianity of Christ."

To be the friend of the one, is of necessity to be the enemy of the other. I love the pure, peaceable, and impartial Christianity of Christ: I therefore hate the corrupt, slave-holding, women-whipping, cradle-plundering, partial and hypocritical Christianity of this land.

American Christianity does not need an Edward Snowden to leak classified information to muckrakers who will tell all in a sensational exposé. Our junk is out there. It has been for some time. Our missionaries were on the slave ships; our endowments were built up by stolen labor. We split denominations to support the Confederacy, blessed a violent Redemption movement, defended Jim Crow, fretted that civil rights preachers had forsaken their "spiritual" calling, and cooperated in the criminalization of people of color, all the while exporting our religion with zeal.

Rwanda, widely celebrated in American churches as the most evangelized nation in Africa, erupted in violence during the spring of 1994. Nearly a million people were massacred by neighbors who'd learned from Christian missionaries the "essential" racial difference between Hutus and Tutsis. Rwanda's genocide began on Thursday of Easter Week. The ghosts of Colfax Courthouse haunt the streets of the Rwandan capital, Kigali.

Such contradictions have not gone unnoticed. They drive the exponential growth of those who, when asked for their religious affiliation, choose "none." (According to the most recent Pew Center data, that's a quarter of all Americans, and over a third of those under the age of thirty-five.)

Why are millennials choosing to part ways with the faith of their parents? No doubt the reasons are many and complex. But one clear factor in the decline of white Christianity is a prevailing sense that Christians are more likely to be racist, homophobic, self-righteous, and blindly patriotic. Not just in the past. And not just in the South. This is the lived experience of twenty-first-century Americans. Theirs is not an angry rebellion against conservative values. It simply seems to them that the Christianity of this land makes people worse.

I get it. Self-righteousness sucks. And we have, all of us, inherited a mess. I don't for a minute blame those who've set out to find a better way, retreated to what seem like safer spaces, or otherwise sought to distance themselves from organized religion. I know how nasty we Christians can be.

But I also keep getting interrupted by Jesus. Twenty years ago, on a sidewalk in Washington, DC, I heard the Jesus who has been interrupting the Christianity of this land since the first slave ships arrived at Jamestown. He was a stranger to me, yet he spoke a language I knew from Scripture and committed to memory. Following him hasn't meant leaving foggy mornings behind. I know this Jesus and love him. But I failed to recognize him right here in my neighborhood for years. Still, the Jesus whom Frederick Douglass trusted doesn't give up on someone like me. This Jesus hasn't given up on any of us. He finds us in our self-deception and interrupts us. He invites us to follow him into a whole new world.

On the Road to Emmaus

At the end of Luke's Gospel, a man named Cleopas walks home after Passover in Jerusalem—after the weekend that Christians remember as Good Friday, Holy Saturday, and Easter Sunday. This good and religious man has made a pilgrimage from Emmaus to his faith's holy city. Maybe he was there among the crowds when they greeted Jesus with palm branches outside Jerusalem singing and shouting because they believed that all they'd ever hoped for was riding into town as the prophet had foretold, "on a colt, the foal of a donkey" (Matthew 21:5). Maybe it was his first pilgrimage. Maybe it was his thirtieth. Whatever the case, he's felt what all those psalms of ascent are about. He's been to the mountaintop.

But that thrill is behind Cleopas now as he makes his way home with an unnamed partner, stumbling blindly into the unknown. Passover is finished. Jesus is dead. Though rumors of the Messiah stirred his spirit, Cleopas is feeling down—sobered, at the very least (how could he have been so naive?), more likely depressed. Foggy mornings can be like that.

His chin on his chest, Cleopas is talking about Judas, who betrayed Jesus—the one who led the temple police to find him in a garden. He's calling the names of religious leaders who condemned Jesus in court, who used their best preaching voices to declare, "We have no king but Caesar!" (John 19:15). He's swapping stories about what Jesus said as he was dying, about who came to claim his body, and about who might have stolen it from the tomb.

These disciples on the road to Emmaus are people whose religious expectations have been interrupted. They're trying to make sense of it all.

In the midst of their conversation, the resurrected Jesus shows up to walk with them. Luke, the storyteller, relishes the dramatic irony. We know long before Cleopas that the Jesus they're grieving is walking alongside them. He's the one asking them about what's going on. Jesus is the one retelling the story of Moses and the Prophets. But Cleopas doesn't know it yet. Cleopas is still reeling from the emotional turmoil of interrupted expectations.

Later, after Jesus has gotten their attention—after these two disciples invite him in as a guest at their table, only to watch him bless and break the bread, becoming their host—Cleopas will exclaim, "Were not our hearts burning within us while he talked with us on the road and opened the Scriptures to us?" (Luke 24:32).

After the fact, looking back, they'll realize that this is what Jesus was doing all along. He was, as he said in John's Gospel, fulfilling the law (John 15:25). In the imagery of Matthew's account, he was reenacting the whole story of God's people, Israel. In the simplicity of Mark's language, he was announcing, Turn around! You're going the wrong way! ("repent," we often translate it; Mark 1:15).

For the first time, Cleopas realizes why Jesus' message had thrilled him: *Jesus was reconstructing the gospel.* He wasn't wielding religion to redeem his people from some imagined enemy or to restore a nostalgic memory of better days. He was, instead, interrupting religion's tendency to turn against itself. Jesus was saving us from ourselves—even from religious sin.

This is the temptation that religion always faces: to reject God's gift by believing that faith is our business to manage, our tool to use on other people or society. As wicked and self-centered as the political powers of his day were, Jesus wasn't killed by political calculation. Pilate said, "I find no fault in this man" (Luke 23:4 KJV). Jesus was killed by an immoral majority who were offended by the way he read the Scriptures and sought to reconstruct their message.

Jesus went to the cross and rose again to reconstruct the gospel. This is what God's movement in the world is always about. So even if we can only make sense of our lives looking back—even if, like Cleopas, we only sense the prophet's fire stirring our hearts after the fact—this recollection is where reconstruction begins for each of us. Every day, a new beginning.

Luke invites me into the dramatic irony of Cleopas's story because he knows that I am Cleopas. I'm still reading this story I was raised on because I'm religious if nothing else. A good sermon still gives me goose bumps. I get up early to sit quietly, listening for God every morning. When no one else is with me on a long car ride, I sing "Great Is Thy Faithfulness" aloud.

Yes, these are the words and songs of a religion that stirred white men to burn down the Colfax Courthouse and kill everyone inside on Easter Sunday. Yes, this is the same Bible slavemasters preached to their slaves, believing it would make them more obedient. Yes, this good news has been turned into very bad news.

But that is not all—because the same Jesus who met Cleopas on the road to Emmaus is here, living and active, walking alongside you and me. Sometimes he's holding a Styrofoam cup, begging us to see him, and sometimes he's holding a sign that says Black Lives Matter, refusing to be ignored. But whenever we are willing to stop and listen—whenever we open ourselves to hear the stories we think we know from a different perspective—there is the possibility that something revolutionary will happen.

The stranger I've been taught to fear sits down at my table, asks the blessing, and breaks the bread. And I'm invited to reread my Bible, to reimagine everything I ever knew. No, I can't dip into the DPAC and get my Christmas-spirit fix in ninety minutes any more. I can't celebrate Easter without remembering the ghosts of Colfax. But when I reread the Scriptures after watching Black Lives Matter illuminate the gospel for young black men in Walltown, I also can't keep from asking you, my fellow traveler, "Were not our hearts burning within us while he opened the Scriptures to us?"

3

RACIAL
BLINDNESS

★

*S**in is a complicated thing for religious people,* even if we have a hard time admitting it to ourselves. We tell our children that the allure of illicit sex or drugs may be enticing but it's really only the devil trying to trick them. All those smiling faces on the cover of *People* magazine—well, deep down they're miserable. Just look at them without all their makeup, there on the tabloid covers in the checkout line. Behind their masks, they're hurting. But they don't know how to find their way out of the mess they're in. When we're looking at someone else, we can see how sin is tricky. Because sin is, at its very root, self-deception.

This is why religious people talk about being saved. Our story teaches us that we would be lost except for the grace that caught us when we could not help ourselves. We constantly remind ourselves and our children that God has given us something we could not have come up with on our own—what the apostle Paul calls "the life that is truly life" (1 Timothy 6:19).

I preach a version of this message every week. I believe it down to my marrow, and I love nothing more than the chance to sit face-to-face with someone who's really listening and talk with them about how Jesus shows us what it looks like to really live. In my enthusiasm, I'll even preach this gospel to preteens who aren't listening (because sometimes they hear something, even when they aren't listening).

A dozen years ago, when I was a young white guy who'd joined an all-black church, I got a call from our summer camp director. He told me the health department had sent someone over to the church to talk with the teenagers about sex, but he thought they should get a biblical perspective as well. Would I come talk with them?

I was glad to. In my own teen years, I'd heard more than enough about the dangers of sex. I wanted to offer these youth a constructive vision—something good and true to look forward to. I wanted to help them see sex as a gift that ultimately points people to God.

I gave them the best stories I could muster on biblical love and faithfulness. I tried to wax eloquent about the true end of marriage. When I finally stopped talking, the kids just stared at me.

I told them they didn't have to agree. I'd love to hear their honest feedback.

Silence.

Finally, a young man spoke up. "Yo, that all sounds good, but I just gotta be real with you. We don't know *anybody* like that."

"Like what?" I asked him.

"Like . . . who got it all together to get married, buy a house, hold down a job, and raise some kids? I mean, you're right. It *would* be nice. But we don't really see it happening."

In the best way I knew how, I'd told those kids the biblical truth. But I knew in that moment that I was missing something. I not only assumed that the good life I imagined as a white man in America was what God wants for everyone, but I also naively suggested that these young people had the freedom to choose biblical faithfulness in all the same ways I did.

Truth was, I didn't have a clue. Here I was preaching grace and the good life, and a young brother who could hardly remember his mother and whose father, I'd later learn, was in prison, was showing me what it looks like to bear ignorance graciously.

In time, those young guys helped me understand that my ignorance began with the false assumption that I could see what was happening around me. I got it honest, of course. The same people who taught me to confess my sins also raised me to think that I should know better.

My false confidence was all tied up with a piety that my religious tradition reinforced rather than challenged. Somehow I'd internalized this idea that being Christian was about knowing what's right.

I thought more about how we often talk about sin. Whenever one of our own "backslide," we explain their fall from grace in ways that assume they knew better. We lament that they've "given in to temptation" or "succumbed to the flesh."

Of course, these things happen. We can't deny that the deacon slept with the alto from choir or that the church secretary was taking a cut from Sunday's offering before she made the bank deposit on Monday morning. Pious Christians aren't blind. We know that people screw up. "For all have sinned and fall short of the glory of God," we say (Romans 3:23). But we like to think sinners *choose* to put momentary pleasure ahead of eternal reward. We like to think people *decide* to live in sin.

Even when we mess up, we like to think we knew what we were doing. But the Christian men who burned down the Colfax Courthouse on Easter Sunday in 1873 and summarily executed forty of their brothers in Christ didn't think they were giving in to temptation. If anything, they fought the temptation to sit out the moral struggle of their day. Their religion didn't temper their violence. It added fuel to the flames.

The religious authorities who arrested Jesus, testified against him, and called for his crucifixion weren't succumbing to the flesh. They were standing up for righteousness. They were doing their religious duty, which is why sin is so complicated for religious people. Because even as we feel guilty about doing the things we know we ought not do and strive to do more of the good we want to do, our very worst sins are almost always things we *know* to be our Christian duty.

Consider the Crusades, the colonization of the Americas, the enslavement and lynching of African Americans, the Holocaust, and the Rwandan genocide. Sadly, the list could go on. Over and over, Christians support and participate in atrocious evil, not because we choose to do wrong but because we think we're doing the right thing—the *righteous* thing even. Like me talking to the neighborhood kids about sex, too often we don't even know what we can't see.

Racial Blindness

The further removed we are from our blindness, the easier it is to think we know better. Distance lets us imagine that we would never have prayed for Hitler's success or killed our Rwandan neighbors with machetes, all while feeling righteous as we work to rid the world of evil.

But nothing calls us into account like sitting face-to-face with our contradictions. I couldn't ignore the kid who called out my racial blindness when we sat down to talk about sex at the neighborhood summer camp. And white evangelicals can't ignore black and brown sisters and brothers in America who ask why 81 percent of us voted in 2016 for a man who was endorsed by the Ku Klux Klan. At least, we can't ignore them if we see them.

The moral contradiction of Donald Trump came up for my family during Easter dinner, when he was still one among many potential Republican nominees in the primary campaign. Our twelve-year-old, JaiMichael, was sitting beside his great-grandfather, enjoying a piece of turkey with cranberry sauce. JaiMichael is African American. His great-grandfather is white.

Trump's promises to build a wall on the Mexican border and ban all Muslims from the country were making headlines. But his appeal made no sense to JaiMichael, who has gone to school with Mexican and Muslim immigrants his whole life. JaiMichael had caught wind that his great-grandfather was sympathetic to candidate Trump. He wanted to know why.

During a lull in the dinner conversation, when everyone at the table could hear, JaiMichael asked, "Are you really going to vote for Trump, Pa?"

"Well, yes, I think so," Pa said.

"But he's *extreme*," JaiMichael replied, his face twisted in confusion.

Pa said something about how politicians have to say things they don't really mean to get elected, and JaiMichael didn't press the issue. He knew his Pa loved him, and he knew Trump's characterization of his friends didn't make sense. JaiMichael couldn't reconcile these two realities. He didn't even try. "Huh," he said. And the conversation moved on.

But a few months later, in the thick of Trump's debates with Hillary Clinton, I got a copy of *Decision* magazine in the mail. It helped me explain to JaiMichael why Pa was going to vote for Trump. It also helped me explain to myself how racial blindness is at the root of so many of our religious contradictions in America.

Because I am a lifelong evangelical, *Decision* magazine, a publication of the Billy Graham Evangelistic Association (BGEA), is part of my culture. Billy Graham invited me to give my life to Jesus at a football stadium when I was ten years old. I read Graham's autobiography, *Just As I Am*, the year it came out (by then, I was sixteen).

Two decades later, my faith has been challenged and stretched by other voices. Still, I'm an evangelical. I read my copy of *Decision* magazine not so much for edification but for some insight into how my family and friends are invited to see the world. Or, sometimes, not to see it.

This special election issue was titled "From Franklin Graham: The Most Important Election of Our Lifetime." In its opening column, Franklin Graham, heir of the Graham mantle, wrote that "if the forces of evil that are allied against the free exercise of our faith succeed," then we as a nation "will devolve into moral anarchy." The 2016 election was, he believed, "the most significant since Abraham Lincoln was chosen to guide a divided country through a bloody and protracted civil war."

This wasn't politics as usual; 2016 was a turning point. Decision 2016 reached beyond the typical partisan differences to fundamental moral concerns, Graham argued. The stakes hadn't been this high since just before the Civil War.

And what moral issues might demand the shedding of American blood in the twenty-first century? What "free exercise" of religion, a promise of the First Amendment to the US Constitution, was under threat?

In multiple articles, *Decision* argued that judicial decisions about equal protection for LGBTQ citizens threatened the practice of Christian faith in America. These court decisions and other pro-LGBTQ actions by the Obama administration were framed as an assault on religious liberty. Franklin Graham sincerely compared the enslavement of African Americans to a conservative being asked to bake a wedding cake for a gay couple or to a guy who might find himself in a bathroom stall next to a man who used to be a woman.

Liberal elites laugh at people like Franklin Graham. His logic seems ridiculous to them. But I could only cry because every white man (and the few women) who wrote an article in that magazine was convinced he or she was taking a stand for Jesus. And in their zeal, they couldn't see how their blindness might hurt people who they and my grandfather genuinely care about.

To JaiMichael, Trump's Klan appeal disqualified him from the start. At twelve, my son could feel the threat of Trump's words to his body. But Pa wasn't endorsing bigotry when he voted for Donald Trump. He didn't want his grandson to be called the n-word at school, and he was genuinely troubled by the surge of hate crimes that followed Trump's victory.

Pa voted for Trump because he believed it was his Christian duty. And sitting beside JaiMichael at Easter dinner did nothing to undermine that. If you asked Pa what the greatest commandment of Scripture is, he would tell you, "Love the Lord your God with all your heart and with all your soul and with all your mind and with all your strength." And he would never fail to mention, as our Lord Jesus taught, that the second commandment is like it: "Love your neighbor as yourself" (Mark 12:30-31).

But Pa and millions of white evangelicals like him didn't turn their backs on their religion to vote against the well-being of black and brown sisters and brothers. They voted for Trump *as an act of faith*, trusting that it was the right thing to do despite the objections of people they know and love—despite their own gut sense that the casino mogul was self-obsessed and dangerous. And *Decision* magazine, along with thousands of blogs, sermons, and newsletters like it, did nothing to question this racial blindness. They encouraged it.

This, more than anything, is the contradiction that white evangelicals in America must face—far too often, our piety looks like sin to people of color who feel they wear their skin like an invisibility cloak before white evangelicals. When the assumptions of whiteness consistently trump the basic demands of evangelical charity, even a twelve-year-old can see that the description doesn't match the fact. Something more powerful than simple logic is at work.

"Who has bewitched you?" Paul asks the foolish Galatians (3:1). I imagine a black boy saying to me, "This 'love your neighbor' bit *sounds* nice. But I don't really see it happening."

How to Lose Your Sight

Nearly two centuries ago, when Christians practiced chattel slavery in this place where I now live, George Freeman pastored Christ Church, Raleigh, a congregation whose building still sits across the street from North Carolina's Old State Capitol. In the fall of 2016, just after I'd received my copy of *Decision* magazine in the mail, Franklin Graham held a rally in the shadow of Christ Church's steeple. This home-state grand finale of the BGEA's $10 million, fifty-state tour was, according to Graham, nonpartisan. Still, he warned those who gathered for prayer that *progressive* was a euphemism for atheist. And he lauded Republican Governor Pat McCrory's Christian values, despite a federal court ruling just months before that found a North Carolina bill had "target[ed] African Americans with almost surgical precision."

As his words echoed off the Christ Church building, Graham argued that Christians had a solemn duty to pray for their nation and vote for candidates who would redeem America from its liberal decline. "We have to stand up and tell them to shut up," he said, "because there are more of us than there are of them."

Graham's math, as it turned out, was off. McCrory, the governor he'd praised, lost his reelection bid by just over ten thousand votes. But Trump won North Carolina handily, a result Graham later attributed to a "God-factor" that the mainstream media had missed. He did not realize how directly his line of reasoning flowed from the Bishop George W. Freeman's *The Rights and Duties of Slave-Holders*, an exhortation written 180 years earlier from the pastor's desk of Christ Church, Raleigh, across the street from where Graham had rallied North Carolina's faithful.

To trace the line from Bishop Freeman to Franklin Graham is to begin to understand why white Christians cannot see sisters and brothers of color in twenty-first-century America. As I listened to Graham and thought about my grandfather, I knew we'd not failed to see because our eyes were closed, like night watchmen asleep at their post. No, Graham spoke with the same stirring conviction that George Washington Freeman felt when he wrote, "I tremble for Christian masters and mistresses throughout the land. . . . Have *any of us 'given'*—to the full extent and meaning of the Apostle's precept, in respect to this, the most important of all their [the enslaved people's] interests—*have we 'given unto our servants that which is just and equal?'"*

To apathetic bystanders, activists often cry, "Wake up! Open your eyes!" But apathy was not the problem for white evangelicals, neither in 1836 nor in 2016. They were wide awake and working tirelessly to enact their vision of redemption.

Freeman referenced the King James Version I memorized as a kid—that text in Colossians where the apostle Paul writes, "Masters, give unto your servants that which is just and equal; knowing that ye also have a Master in heaven" (Colossians 4:1). Across the Atlantic Ocean, where London was still the center of world power, slavery had recently been abolished. Amid the spiritual fervor of America's Second Great Awakening, the American Antislavery Society was communicating a consistent and clear interpretation of the apostle: *the only "just and equal" way to treat a slave was to free him.* Faced with a deluge of petitions for abolition during its 1836 session, the US House of Representatives adopted a gag rule, which immediately tabled any legislation calling for an end to slavery.

This was the context in which Freeman wrote about the rights and duties of slaveholders. Like Graham and other white evangelicals who lamented the rampant "immorality" throughout the administration of America's first black president, Freeman did not explicitly attack abolitionists or any political opponent. Instead, he appealed to nostalgia. "My brethren, I am but bringing again to light, that which was once well understood and uniformly practiced . . . but which has, I regret to say, been greatly obscured, and, indeed, almost lost sight of, in this our day." Freeman steered religion toward one great end: to make America great again.

And he did it not by asking Christians to shirk their faith but by challenging them to fulfill it more faithfully. What did the slaveholder owe his slaves? Not liberty, but evangelism, Freeman claimed. "*Have they* not immortal souls?" he asked, exhorting plantation owners to take personal responsibility for the salvation of the people they enslaved. "As Providence has placed them in a situation in which they are more immediately dependant [sic] upon us, so we are made more *directly responsible for their moral and religious improvement.*"

The single force that people confessed to be greater than any earthly power was thus employed to reinforce the status quo. The God who raised Israel up out of Egypt was not working to deliver African Americans from slavery to freedom as the abolitionists so impudently insisted. He was, instead, creator of an institution in which people of color are subject to white rule. "Their state of pupilage *never ceases*," Freeman wrote. As this god would have it, white men are responsible for maintaining order.

In a world so conceived, white people could not see black sisters and brothers who knelt beside them at the Communion rail. They looked at women who had in some cases changed their diapers and saw ignorant children who could not possibly understand how the world really works.

While a lot has changed in 180 years, the basic paternalism Freeman assumed still energizes Franklin Graham and many evangelicals who, like him, have inherited the patterns of slaveholder religion. In March of 2012, when Barack Obama was running for reelection, Franklin Graham agreed to meet with a delegation of African American clergy from North Carolina's NAACP. The ministers had written Graham, expressing concern about his public attacks on President Obama's personal faith. Sitting together at a dinner that the BGEA hosted, Graham listened to his African American sisters and brothers. He nodded his head as they invited him to reconsider what he thought he knew about how the world works and what it means to do our Christian duty. Then he smiled and asked if they'd like a tour of the facilities.

Like Freeman at the Communion rail, Graham thought he knew better. Like Pa at Easter dinner, his religion compelled him to do his Christian duty. Four years later, Graham crisscrossed the country tirelessly exhorting overwhelmingly white crowds outside every state capitol in America to vote their values. When they did, the Ku Klux Klan held a victory parade in Roxboro, North Carolina, just up the road from where I live.

You Have to Want to See

At the center of Mark's Gospel, Jesus' message is framed by two stories about blind men receiving their sight. These stories serve as a window through which Jesus' healing and teaching are revealed. Like a refrain in a well-crafted poem, they sum up the heart of Jesus' message.

Through these stories, Mark asserts that the gospel is about learning to see, which, in its own way, speaks to our most basic problem. Sin is a kind of blindness. In order to show us, his readers, what we cannot see on our own, Mark invites us to observe how Jesus restores sight to two blind men.

The first man is led by the hand, as blind people often are, to Jesus. Word has gotten out. Jesus can make the blind to see again.

Taking this unnamed man by the hand, Jesus becomes his guide. He walks him to the edge of town, spits on his eyes, and asks, "Do you see anything?" (Mark 8:23).

Yes, the man can see people. But by his own account "they look like trees walking around" (Mark 8:24). His sight is blurry. So Jesus touches him a second time, and he sees everything clearly.

Two chapters later, Mark introduces a second blind man, Bartimaeus. This time, the one who cannot see is shouting, "Have mercy on me!" (Mark 10:47). Because he cannot see, he is willing to break protocol—to face the rebukes of those who tell him to sit down and shut up—because he wants to see. No one leads Bartimaeus to Jesus. He throws off his cloak and runs to him.

And there before the crowd—before the whole audience of Mark's life work and *the good news about Jesus*—Jesus asks Bartimaeus the most basic question of the human heart: "What do you want?" (Mark 10:51). This is the question Jesus has been trying to get his disciples to grapple with. They've seen his power. They've believed his message. They've left everything to follow him. But "what good is it for someone to gain the whole world, yet forfeit their soul?" Jesus asks them (Mark 8:36).

What do you really want?

Before encountering Bartimaeus, Jesus has responded to a rich young ruler. After the tragic encounter with the young ruler, Jesus tells the disciples, "Many who are first will be last, and the last first" (Mark 10:31). And then, when they think they've turned from worldly success to pursue a seat beside their Lord in his coming kingdom, Jesus challenges them again: "Whoever wants to be first must be slave of all" (Mark 10:44).

What do you really want?

Bartimaeus isn't just answering this question for himself. As Mark tells it, he's answering for the disciples and the crowds and the religious leaders—for all of us who are blind, even if we don't know we cannot see.

What do you want? Jesus asks him.

"Rabbi, I want to see" (Mark 10:51).

Of all the prophetic words in Scripture, Bartimaeus's simple confession may be the most damning of slaveholder religion and its habits, which have been passed down to us. If we are honest to God and ourselves, we have not wanted to see. Far too often, we have chosen blindness, even refusing the hands of friends who reached out and tried to lead us to the one who could restore our sight.

Our racial blindness is generational and multilayered, folded in among all that is true and good about our faith. There is no easy way to be freed from it.

Thanks to the work of psychologists, we know a lot more about racial blindness today than we did two decades ago. In the late 1990s, Anthony Greenwald, a professor of psychology at the University of Washington, developed an instrument called the Implicit Association Test to quantify how people associate the race they perceive with how they feel about other people. Millions have taken the test online through Project Implicit. I took it again myself recently, fully aware that it was measuring my implicit racial bias. But despite racial blindness being the first thing on my mind, I still demonstrated a "slight preference" for white people. This is overwhelmingly the case for most people who take the test—a sample set of the population that, like readers of this book, is probably less likely than the average American to harbor any conscious bias against another person or group based on race.

But there it is. The data say I can't autocorrect in real time for the very blindness I'm trying to recover from. I'm like Bartimaeus, running toward Jesus, hands out to catch me if I trip and fall in the darkness that surrounds me. Still, I find hope in the way this gospel story shows us that all freedom begins with us wanting it.

You have to want to see.

The desire itself is the interruption that can save us. As long as we sacrifice ourselves to a false sense of duty—fighting for what we already know to be good and true—we are captive to the spirit of men who held other people captive. But if we let our guard down—if we can but allow ourselves to be present with the real people in our lives, we can learn to want new things. All desire is bodily. If we can sit down to eat together, we can take in not only the food we long for but also the fellowship we so deeply need.

In the early 1800s, when he was growing up in the same North Carolina where George Freeman would preach evangelization to slaveholders and Franklin Graham would declare progressives atheist, a young white boy named Levi Coffin watched people who looked like him march enslaved African Americans down the road in front of his house. These men had run away to freedom, Coffin later learned, but the laws of the United States allowed slave catchers to capture and return them to bondage. Coffin was troubled by what he saw, and he never forgot it. Following the Jesus he first met in a Quaker meeting house outside of Greensboro, North Carolina, Coffin went on to devote his life to abolition, becoming the unofficial "President of the Underground Railroad" before his death in 1877. By grace, Coffin learned to see.

Yes, you have to want to see—and hundreds of years of history have hammered into our psyches a desire for what we imagine to be "white." But as long as Jesus eats with the disciples and brother Franklin Graham sits down for dinner with the NAACP and Pa shares Easter dinner with JaiMichael, there is the possibility that we can learn to want something more. Maybe we even learn that our true Christian duty is to see and want one another.

4

LIVING IN SKIN

★

Those boys who stared back in silence after my sex talk at the summer camp—they didn't give up on the white preacher who'd landed in their neighborhood. As they could see, I was blind. But I wanted to learn to see. So they took me by the hand and walked me out to the edge of a world I'd thought I understood. They decided to help a brother out.

Mario told me I needed to listen to some Tupac. "Alright," I said. "Let me hear his best stuff."

I didn't tell Mario that, where I grew up, people who were saved didn't listen to rap music. I'd been saved since before I knew how to turn a radio dial. Not listening to 102 JAMZ wasn't something anyone ever explained to me. It was a given—like locking our doors when we drove through East Winston or scoffing at anything that smacked of big government. Our silent boycott of a whole genre of music couldn't have had anything to do with the fact that rap was "black music." We weren't like that. I knew from an early age that I was a colorblind Christian.

Besides, Vanilla Ice was one of the most notorious of the bad-boy rappers—and he was white.

Before I met Mario, it never occurred to me that I might be missing out on something by cutting myself off from the entire world of rap music. But I had begun to realize that my piety had its own contradictions. Like the fact that every church deacon I ever rode along with to the tobacco market played Garth Brooks on the truck radio. About the time I hit puberty, I started to feel why a man might want to "slip on down to the oasis" and meet up with some "friends in low places." Rappers, it turned out, weren't the only entertainers who played to human passion. But those urges, I knew, had to be resisted—at least until marriage. That's what they taught us in the True Love Waits program.

I don't recall the preacher's name, but we watched him on videos at our weekly Fellowship of Christian Athletes meetings. (Half the guys I played basketball with were black, but I don't ever recall a conversation at the FCA about why we were an all-white group.) Our True Love Waits preacher had a megachurch somewhere down in Texas, with a big, open stage where he paced back and forth like Garth Brooks live, but without the cowboy hat. The preacher held his Bible out in front of him, open to the Song of Songs, and translated all the adulation of human anatomy and descriptions of sex positions into Southern vernacular. Anyone trying to figure out how to get young people out for Bible study should go back and dig up those videos. I never missed a week.

His main point was a good one, and it stuck with me—God made bodies. Our bodies are a gift. Too much Christianity is about denying the body to save the spirit, but the Song of Songs is all about our bodies and the joy of sex pointing us to God.

Though I couldn't provide the whole stage performance of those videos, this was the idea I'd hoped to get across when I sat down to talk with Mario and his friends about sex. It had been good news to me when I was their age. I assumed it would ring true to them.

But my racial blindness kept me from seeing that Mario and his friends weren't out of touch with their bodies. Far from it. They were young men trying to learn how to survive in black bodies that felt threatened every day.

It wasn't that I didn't want to see Mario. It wasn't even that I couldn't perceive him there in front of me as a fellow human being, created in the image of God. No, it was more that he and his friends looked "like trees walking around." I didn't have any capacity to comprehend their reality.

And my faith was little help because I had received and interpreted it through the experience of other white Americans—which is why Mario knew I needed Tupac. A natural poet, Tupac both knew the world Mario was trying to navigate and could describe it with dramatic power that made Pastor True-Love-Waits seem blasé. If anyone could paraphrase the Song of Songs in America, it was Tupac: "Fingertips on the hips as I dip / Gotta get a tight grip" (a relatively G-rated line from his corpus). No one needed to help this brother get in touch with bodily passion.

Tupac seemed to know instinctively what Scripture assumes: that the way to God and truth is not away from flesh but through it. Mario played Tupac's "Keep Ya Head Up" for me, insisting that this was the purest distillation of his vision. "Some say the blacker the berry, the sweeter the juice," he began, over top of Tupac's track. "I say the darker the flesh, then the deeper the roots." I watched a smile stretch Mario's cheeks as he closed his eyes and savored a good line, turning his face toward the sun. Here was a message that kissed his soul.

I did a little reading to learn Tupac's backstory. His mother, Afeni Shakur, had been born Alice Faye Williams, just down the road in Lumberton, North Carolina. Growing up under Jim Crow in the South, she learned the freedom songs of the civil rights movement and went on to join the Black Panther Party, determined to use the power she and her community had to protect their children—the bodies of Tupac and Mario and millions like them. Tupac was rapping to his mama when he exhorted, "Keep Ya Head Up." He was honoring her life of sacrifice when he observed, "the darker the flesh, then the deeper the roots." Yes, she'd been through hell in her dark flesh—more often than not *because* of its hue. But she'd also shown him what faithfulness looks like. Afeni Shakur and millions like her deserved to stand tall, with their heads up. Tupac's music told Mario he could look to the sun and know that joy of God kissing his black face.

Whether he knew it or not, Mario spit Tupac's rhymes into Southern soil for me, offering the mud of conversation as a healing balm for my blurry sight, as Jesus had done for the blind man at Bethsaida. It didn't happen all at once. It took time. But I kept listening, kept watching, and eventually I started to see: *my problem as a white man was that I didn't know how to live in skin.* This was the poverty of my so-called privilege, what kept me from seeing the fullness of the gospel's power for my own life, for Mario, and for the rest of God's good world.

I remembered a white professor at the Christian liberal arts school where I studied philosophy holding forth in a seminar on Allan Bloom's *The Closing of the American Mind* about the corrosive effects of rap music on young minds. "You may not fully realize this because you lack *the experience*," he opined, "but the very beat of rap music is the rhythm of sex." For him, it went without saying that this was a bad thing. But he was no poet. Tupac understood how any art that echoes the rhythm of life is simply human.

Through Tupac's music, Mario helped me see that a faith that keeps you from living in your own skin can only make you less human.

American Slavery and the Problem of Bodies

America's original sin of race-based slavery is rooted in our bodies. While most of us will do what we can to save our own skin, our bodies bear the curse of human rebellion—the sweat of the brow and the pains of labor. The sins of our fathers (and mothers) bear down on bent backs and sciatic nerves.

Slavery has always been one means humans employ to skirt this curse. To the victor belong the spoils is an ancient truism of war. Often in human history the spoils included people. But war is not the only way some bodies became subject to others. In the opening lines of the exodus story, the Bible says "a new king, to whom Joseph meant nothing, came to power in Egypt" (Exodus 1:8). In the messiness of politics, favor comes and goes. But the people who are in power almost always make sure someone else carries the weight and does the dirty work.

The unique contribution of slavery during the establishment of the American colonies was the employment of skin color to assign a class of people to perpetual servitude. Originally, white and black people came to the colonies as servants of the settler class, but race-based slavery emerged as an efficient means of building up the plantation economy by permanently assigning people of African descent to the status of slave. Africans who survived the long journey across the Atlantic Ocean, often chained to one another and packed prostrate in the hold of a ship, became human chattel in the New World. In explicit contrast to the enslavable black flesh of Africans, people of European descent began to imagine themselves as *white*. By virtue of their whiteness—and for no other reason—they imagined a divine right to own black bodies.

For the people whose sable skin rendered them subject to use and abuse, this arrangement was obviously anathema. "And before I'd be a slave / I'd be buried in my grave / and go home to my Lord and be free," they sang when white folks weren't listening. Tactics of resistance varied, but people of African descent always knew in their bodies the basic heresy of race-based slavery.

And *in their bodies*, white people knew it too. To comprehend the moral contradiction of America's original sin, you must consider what it meant for a young, white man to come of age on a plantation. Imagine yourself growing up amid a pastoral landscape in the early nineteenth century, a half-day's horse ride from the closest city. As for any child, your world is the people you've known and the places familiar to you since birth—the Big House, which you've always called home, and the barn where your daddy tied a rope swing from the rafters so you could fly down from the loft and land safely in that mound of hay by the horse stalls. For as long as you can remember, you've always had your studies and your chores to do. Mother always insisted that you learn responsibility. But you always felt closer to Betsy, the enslaved black woman who changed your diapers and cooked your food and picked you up when you fell and skinned your knees. You never remember running down to the barn to play without Betsy's two boys and Imogene, the girl between them—the one that was born just three months after you.

For you, a son of so-called privilege, puberty means beginning to make sense of why you kissed Imogene down in the hay pile when y'all were six and why you both always knew you could never tell a soul. It means coming to terms with the fact that you and Imogene both share your father's nose. And it means beginning to internalize an arrangement in which you will one day inherit as property the woman who both competed with your mother for your father's love and nursed you at her breast. If you were a good Episcopalian, as most plantation families were, this is also about the time you would be confirmed as a living member of the body of Jesus Christ.

"Now at one's feet there are chasms that had been invisible until this moment," the Southern writer Lillian Smith wrote a century after slavery's end. Describing an experience shared in silence by generations of white Christians, she observed how "one knows, and never remembers how it was learned, that there will always be chasms, and now across the chasms will always be those one loves."

To observe that race-based chattel slavery was a gut-wrenching experience that white people also experienced *in their bodies* is not in any way to equate their suffering with that of African Americans. It is, instead, to try to understand the lived experience that informed the ways they read the Bible and imagined their world. Because even though slavery ended in 1865, most white Christians went on reading the Bible and seeing the world around them exactly as they had before.

Growing up Southern Baptist in North Carolina, I memorized Scripture in the King James Version and engaged in a serious program of discipleship as a white adolescent without ever giving serious consideration to the *Southern* in our denomination's name. Then in 1995, the summer before my freshman year of high school, the Southern Baptist Convention (SBC) issued an official apology for its endorsement of slavery. There it was. We'd separated ourselves from our American Baptist sisters and brothers some 150 years earlier in order to stay "Southern" and keep our slaves. Enough water had passed under the bridge for our elders to decide that it was time to bury that hatchet. They said they were sorry.

But their concession stirred up old fears. Before I had finished high school, a conservative movement within the denomination insisted we had become too liberal, took over the denomination, and forced everyone who worked for the International Mission Board to sign a statement of faith to which they added an article about female submission. It was the first time in my life I'd seen people on the local evening news being interviewed about my church.

I remember a professor from the local university explaining how the text from Ephesians that SBC leaders were quoting as a basis for their insistence on female submission was, in fact, one of the primary texts apologists for slavery had quoted in the mid-nineteenth century. "Slaves, obey your earthly masters" (Ephesians 6:5) followed right on the heels of "Wives, submit yourselves to your own husbands as you do to the Lord" (Ephesians 5:22). The opening line of the whole passage was glossed over in both cases: "Submit to one another out of reverence for Christ" (Ephesians 5:21).

It was a ten-second spot on the evening news, but it touched me deeply. They were talking about my people and how we read our Bible. I studied Greek and Hebrew and went to seminary, in part, because I wanted to learn to see. A decade of education taught me a lot, but it took Mario spitting rhymes on the curb to really open my eyes.

Being out of touch with my own body kept me from reading the Bible well. And this wasn't just a personal problem. It was part of the collective psyche that came with assuming I was white. It was the implicit bias that could be measured but couldn't simply be erased. It was the patterns of whiteness I simply had not noticed: a lifetime of attending all-white Bible studies, locking the car doors in predominantly black neighborhoods, assuming my white professors knew what they were talking about, and silently boycotting rap music. Racial blindness was in my spiritual DNA.

If Adam and Eve ate the apple, infecting us all with sin, I wanted to know who in my lineage had taken away my sight. I read that Thornton Stringfellow, pastor of the Stevensburg Baptist Church in Virginia, had made one of the most popular arguments for slavery when Baptists in the mid-nineteenth century were deciding to secede from the American Baptist fold. In a university archive, I found a copy of Stringfellow's *A Brief Examination of Scripture Testimony on the Institution of Slavery*. I pored over it like a cancer patient might read her oncology report.

Stringfellow did what Christians have always done to justify injustice. He assumed that the status quo was normal. Abraham, the father of our faith, owned slaves. So did New Testament Christians. Jesus himself had not condemned the practice so it must have been acceptable. Stringfellow, like many before him, read in the curse of Noah's son, Ham, a divine cause for the race-based subjugation that had become a matter of law in America.

But Rev. Stringfellow was haunted by the moral argument of abolitionists. The organized coalition of free blacks, Quakers, and white evangelicals who were on fire for justice had only just begun to speak out when Bishop Freeman wrote his treatise "The Rights and Duties of Slave-Holders" in the mid-1830s. But by 1850, when Stringfellow took up his pen, their moral courage had created a movement. Hundreds of people who knew they were not property had risked life and limb, trusting hearsay that the Underground Railroad could carry them to freedom. With little more than a Bible, a pistol, and moss on the north side of a tree, Harriet Tubman would eventually lead as many as five hundred souls to freedom.

As formerly enslaved people, such as Frederick Douglass and Sojourner Truth, shared publicly about their experience of life in bondage, white Christians began to feel in public life the gut-wrenching moral contradiction they had only considered in private. Ministers like Rev. Stringfellow took it upon themselves to ease the conscience of white congregants by helping them feel good about themselves. He concluded his defense of slavery by asserting that not only was it defensible but it was a great good for Christianity.

Stringfellow claimed with rhetorical flourish that slavery "has brought within the range of Gospel influence, millions of Ham's descendants among ourselves, who, but for this institution, would have sunk down to eternal ruin; knowing not God, and strangers to the Gospel." He went on to argue that enslaved people would probably live better lives in America than they would have as free peasants in Africa. But the truth of his claim hardly mattered because he had, by his very logic, severed his gospel from the real, bodily conditions in which people live.

Because his so-called gospel prioritized the eternal security of souls above the temporal living conditions of bodies, Stringfellow simply could not see the inherent connection between bodies and souls.

This couldn't simply be the way he imagined enslaved people. The logic of Stringfellow's argument reveals how the enslavement of human beings led to a Christianity that struggles to this day with the challenge of reconciling soul and body for all people.

Even though Jesus took on flesh for my sake, whiteness prevents me from knowing how to live in my own skin. And I'm not alone. What's more, my struggle to connect soul and body on the personal level mirrors a struggle I share with millions on the societal level. Even though Jesus proclaimed the advent of a new political reality—the kingdom of God—we consistently fail to connect faith and politics in meaningful, consistent ways. Instead, we Christians who think we are white vacillate between naive nationalism and a pseudospiritual disavowal of politics. Not only do we not know how to live in skin, we're often not clear about what it means to live in the world. We see, as Paul said, "through a glass, darkly" (1 Corinthians 13:12 KJV). Which is to say, everyone looks "like trees walking around."

How Long Has This Been Happening?

Sandwiched between the two stories of blind men receiving their sight, Mark's Gospel presents Jesus as a healer who helps us all to see. Yes, the literally blind, but also the self-righteous and self-centered—from excited crowds who weren't quite clear that Jesus was the Messiah to the disciples who couldn't see what Jesus was really about.

Yes, Jesus gives sight to the blind. But we all have to admit our own blindness—even those of us who have pledged to follow him.

Right in the middle of these stories about learning to see, Mark introduces a father who wants Jesus to heal his son's sick body (Mark 9:14-29). This dad is not spiritually starstruck in the way so many religious people are when they come to see a healer. He's heard about Jesus, but when Jesus is unavailable, dad asks the disciples to attend to his son's body. Like a parent in the emergency room, he just wants help. This dad begs someone— anyone—to drive out the evil spirit. But the disciples are not able to heal his boy's body.

So dad waits for Jesus. "Teacher, I brought you my son, who is possessed by a spirit that has robbed him of speech," he explains. "Whenever it seizes him, it throws him to the ground. He foams at the mouth, gnashes his teeth and becomes rigid" (Mark 9:17-18).

Rather than answer the dad, Jesus replies to the whole "unbelieving generation" (Mark 9:19), expressing exasperation that, because of a lack of trust, the healing that he wants to bring to the world is scarce. Jesus is frustrated. Maybe he wishes the disciples had been able to handle this case on their own. Maybe he's disappointed that God's long relationship with Israel hasn't resulted in greater faith. Maybe, all these years after the initial breach with Adam and Eve, Jesus is lamenting humanity's general condition.

Whatever the case, Jesus is angry when he asks the dad to bring his child to him. In the Hebrew of the Jewish Scriptures, to be "slow to anger" is literally to be "long in the nostrils." Like the image of a red-faced bull with smoke billowing from its nostrils, the Scriptures Jesus read acknowledged anger as a natural, bodily response. His anger is not hasty, petty, or destructive. Rather, it focuses his attention on the true source of this boy's sickness—the root of our common ailment.

What evil spirit has left us out of touch with our bodies?

Any parent with a sick child wants the child to be well, just as those who recognize their blindness want to see. Experiencing my own racial blindness, I want to learn to see. But Jesus' way of healing is not hurried. Rather than simply treat the symptom, Jesus orders more tests. And not just on the boy. He wants to diagnose the whole "unbelieving generation."

When the boy falls down on the dirt in front of him, convulsing, Jesus does not reach out with a healing touch. An immediate crisis does not compel Jesus to hurry up. Instead, he asks dad—and all of us—a question: "How long has he been like this?" (Mark 9:21).

The first time I went to an African American funeral, before the service had even begun, a daughter of the deceased threw herself on her mother's body, wailing. "Don't go! Don't leave me, mama!" she cried. It seemed she thought she could scream loud enough to wake her embalmed mother from the dead.

I did not know what to do as I watched that woman scream, but I distinctly remember feeling that I had to do something. Just like when I imagine that boy convulsing in front of Jesus something inside me says, "Do something!"

But Jesus does not imagine himself as a white man who always has the answer to whatever problem presents itself. He is instead, as Scripture tell us, the Great Physician who searches our souls and sees us with greater clarity than an MRI.

"How long has he been like this?" the Doctor asks. A diagnostic question serves to clarify where treatment must begin. "From childhood," dad answers. This problem has been here from the start.

When Christians confess that sin is original, we are neither blaming God nor condemning ourselves. We are, like the dad in this narrative, simply stating the truth about our condition. We've been this way from the start. Which is to say, our brokenness is an inextricable part of who we've imagined ourselves to be. This is as true for a nation as it is for a single soul.

To confess that racism is America's original sin is not simply to acknowledge that slaves came over on the same ships that carried the missionaries and the political ideals that were eventually written down in America's founding documents. We all know this is true. But anyone who asks in the midst of a particular racial crisis, "How long have we been like this?" is likely to be accused of simply stoking the fires of racial resentment.

Yes, the Middle Passage was terrible. But what does it have to do with Freddie Gray's fatal journey through Baltimore's streets in the back of a paddy wagon? To the racially blind, the answer is nothing. A black man arrested for breaking the law is subject to arrest. If he is mistreated by law enforcement, the law can be trusted to protect his rights and bring charges against the officers. And when the court does not convict? Then Gray's death is either a tragedy or its own kind of justice. "Maybe he shouldn't have been hanging out with that crowd in the first place," somebody says.

But what if Jesus doesn't let you look away? What if he doesn't let you fix anything? What if he looks at you and asks, "How long has it been like this?"

Many white people would rather do something to address the symptoms we can see than acknowledge our original sin. Racism isn't only a part of who we've been. It is, in ways we don't even comprehend, who we are. It has cut us to our very core, severing soul from body. Which is to say, if we are honest with ourselves, we carry the wounds of white supremacy in our bodies.

How long has it been like this? How long have we taught our boys not to cry while not understanding the tears that flow uncontrollably when we least expect them? How long have we defended the integrity of family values in public while being privately confused about the urges that drive us back to Internet porn, searching for an intimacy we can't quite imagine? How long have we asked a woman to "submit herself graciously" while ignoring the obvious signs of domestic abuse in our churches? How long have we scrambled to make it look like our homes and work are in control while worrying deep down that we can't even control ourselves?

White people know these ghosts haunt us, but for all our education and therapy we rarely get to the root of our trouble with living in skin. When desperation leads us to Jesus, we cannot help but ask, like the desperate father, "But if you can do anything, take pity on us and help us."

"Everything is possible for one who believes," Jesus replies.

"I do believe," we confess. "Help me overcome my unbelief!" (Mark 9:22-24).

Sarah Grimké, the daughter of a slaveholder and judge in Charleston, South Carolina, was five years old in 1797 when the sight of an enslaved person being whipped seared her conscience. Like many white people before and after her, she was troubled in her body. It made her sick to her stomach. But Grimké was told this was how the world works. She was supposed to get used to it.

Instead, Grimké read voraciously in her father's law library, trying to understand how it had become normal for white people to own and control black bodies. For over thirty years, she continued to question her privilege and the customs of plantation life. In defiance of South Carolina law, she taught the enslaved woman who worked most closely with her in her father's house to read. When she was thirty-six years old, Grimké finally fled her father's house and native South to become an abolitionist in Philadelphia.

Eight years later, Grimké wrote in an open letter to Southern clergy that "slavery has . . . trampled the image of God in the dust." She was challenging fellow Christians to face what had become clear to her after nearly four decades of personal struggle. Trusting her gut and asking hard questions, Grimké learned to see.

Lord, I do believe. Please help my unbelief.

5

THIS IS MY BODY, BROKEN

★

I *have Mario and the boys at the summer camp* to thank for helping Jesus diagnose my spiritual need to slow down and learn how to live in my skin. Their very real and bodily presence shook me from a spiritual slumber that might well have cost me more than I had any capacity to measure at the time. They helped me along the journey toward becoming a human being in the movement that the Bible calls "church."

But I needed a lot more help, and I found much of what my soul was aching for on my neighbor's porch. Back before Leah and I had kids, after the dinner dishes had been washed and put away each evening, we would sometimes take a walk to get a little exercise and catch up on our day. If we went down the hill from the house where we were living at the time, we passed Ms. Carolyn's porch. She was almost always sitting in her rocking chair alongside one or two other neighbors.

Sometimes the stoop to her porch was already full of people when we passed by.

Ms. Carolyn would always greet us, and we would respond. Sometimes she'd ask a question. Eventually, I realized she was inviting us to sit down and join her little circle. This was a community meeting. And though I didn't know it at first, my neighbors had inherited this practice of porch sitting from generations before them as a means of staying sane.

Porch sitting was, no doubt, its own way of coping with traumatic stress—what some in the African American community call DOTS (daily ongoing traumatic stress, as opposed to the PTSD, post-traumatic stress disorder, that continues to affect people years after an experience of trauma). Here on Ms. Carolyn's porch, neighbors gossiped and laughed about each other, assessed our surroundings, and argued about what was really going on in the world and what any of us could do about it. It wasn't always a circle of perfect love, but it was shared, intergenerational support for folks who didn't try to act like they had it all together. As our kids grew up, they learned there was a candy jar on the little table beside Ms. Carolyn's chair. Even when adults were in the midst of heated discussion, they were welcome to it.

Over the years, what happened in that space revealed itself to be a truer experience of church than almost anything I experienced in a house of worship. This was something of a mystery to me until I visited the restored slave quarters at Stagville, the largest plantation in North Carolina at the end of the Civil War—the one that was owned by members of the Episcopal church where the priest helped me name the experience of racism tearing my soul in two.

For the most part, the storytelling at historic plantations hasn't done much to heal America's racial divide. Go down the magnolia-lined driveway of dozens of Big Houses in the South, and you're likely to find a retired white woman who is eager to show you the china in the dining room and tell you how, in this particular place, slaves were treated better than most. I know from experience that this happens at the Stagville State Historic Site, which is maintained by the state of North Carolina and staffed largely by volunteers.

But on this particular visit, when I took my kids out there with a friend of ours who grew up as the thirteenth son of sharecroppers in South Carolina, we met a young African American woman who was studying history at the University of North Carolina, and she offered to take us down to the slave cabins. On a dirt road, beyond a similar structure where an African American family lived until the 1950s, the historic society has preserved a two-story cabin that was designed in the mid-nineteenth century to house as many as forty people, one family to a room. Our guide, who had read through WPA interviews with the formerly enslaved people who lived here, walked us over to the chimney on the outside of the cabin and showed us where, preserved in the handmade clay bricks, we could see the fingerprints of one of those men.

"Wow," my daughter said, as she placed her finger in the imprint. She was feeling the same thing I'd felt the first time an elder at our church stood up during Black History Month and told us the stories his grandmother had told him about growing up in slavery. Chattel slavery is not ancient history in America. Sometimes, it's close enough to touch. We all carry in our bodies stories that haven't been told.

But that day out at the slave cabin, one of the kids asked an obvious enough question: In a home without a kitchen, where did people eat? From the interviews she had read, our grad student guide sketched a daily routine in which grandma stayed back at the cabins with the small children while able-bodied family members worked the fields. At the end of the day, when everyone came home, the whole community carried their large cooking pots from the outdoor fire grandma had tended to a clearing in the woods where everyone would sit together and talk about their day.

I looked down to the space underneath the trees and imagined that grandma, ladling soup, watching over her family and holding court like Ms. Carolyn. This was their porch, I realized. Coming here was what kept them sane.

In her Nobel Prize–winning novel *Beloved*, Toni Morrison describes such a scene as the "clearing," where matriarch Baby Suggs invites a community of the formerly enslaved together to sing and dance, weep and moan. "She did not tell them to clean up their lives or to go and sin no more," Morrison writes, aware of the spiritual significance of what happened in the brush arbors of plantations, where the slave church was born. "She told them that the only grace they could have was the grace they could imagine. That if they could not see it, they would not have it."

A balm to heal the wounds inflicted by white supremacy, I came to see, was inscribed in the habits of Baby Suggs's descendants—women like Ms. Carolyn, who gathered her community on the porch. When she invited us to join them, she did more to heal the wound in my soul than any number of therapy sessions ever could. Like the Great Physician the Gospels describe, she reached out and offered a hand to lead us into a new way of living.

Racial Habits of the Heart

The difference between the therapeutic religion of mainstream American Christianity and the embodied grace of Ms. Carolyn's porch hangs on the relationship between bodies in these two very different spaces. It's not so much about ideas, really. Our problem isn't that white churches are full of racists while the mixed crowd on Ms. Carolyn's porch is some sort of enlightened remnant of experts in cultural sensitivity. Far from it. You'll hear the n-word on Ms. Carolyn's porch long before you'll hear it slip past the lips of a Bible study leader at the all-white Southern Baptist church downtown. But again, the difference isn't so much about ideas as it is about bodies.

White supremacy doesn't persist because racists scheme to privilege some while discriminating against others. It continues because, despite the fact that almost everyone believes it is wrong to be racist, the daily habits of our bodily existence continue to repeat the patterns of white supremacy at home, at school, at work, and at church. White supremacy is written into our racial habits. In short, it looks like normal life.

With our desires shaped by everything from Barbie dolls to beauty pageants, white boys fall in love with white girls, as our parents did before us. Raising our kids, we teach them to treat everyone fairly, then pass our wealth on to them according to the laws of the land. Thus white wealth is perpetuated without any hint of racism—and the gap between the median incomes of whites and blacks in America remains the same as it was before the civil rights movement.

The same thing happens in our integrated public schools (not to mention our increasingly privatized resegregated ones). White boys, who look like models of genius such as Albert

Einstein or Bill Gates, receive consistent praise from their teachers. With overdeveloped egos, they may struggle to ask for help when we need it or to work well with our peers. But all of this turns out to be an advantage on the "level ground" of an open market, where a white man with a criminal record is more likely to get a job than a similarly qualified black man without one.

Of course, the same black man is six times more likely to get stopped and searched by the police, despite the documented fact that all races use drugs at roughly the same rate. Odds being what they are, a young black man born after 2000 has a one-in-three chance of going to prison at some point in his life. So, as Michelle Alexander has pointed out in her work on *The New Jim Crow*, more black men are in bondage in the United States today than were in slavery in 1850. And almost no one harbors any racial animosity while these disparities persist—because the lie of race isn't an idea anymore; it's a habit.

The systemic nature of racial inequality is complex, and we will come back to it in the next chapter, when we turn to the brokenness of our body politic. But long before we get to public policy, the bald fact of inequality exposes how white supremacy is ultimately about who we love and who we listen to, who we long to be with and how we interact with the so-called other. It's about the patterns of our daily life and the desires that are tied up in them.

And for Christians, these racial habits are often most pronounced in the patterns of our community life—what we usually refer to as "church." Though schools, work, and even many homes saw considerable racial integration in the latter half of the twentieth century, eleven o'clock on Sunday morning has remained, as Dr. King said, America's most segregated hour.

For any Bible-believing American who is heartbroken by racial strife and offended by the crude bigotry of the alt-right, this is a serious reality to grapple with. Everything we know to be true suggests that this is wrong and that Jesus is the answer. But the gospel of white evangelicals hasn't interrupted our racial habits; it has reinforced them.

To be white and Christian in America is to be, on average, more segregated than your unchurched neighbors, whatever the color of their skin. How could this be? The heresy of America's segregated church is rooted in the racial habits of the heart that grew out of the nineteenth century's struggle with America's original sin. From Richard Allen's congregation in Philadelphia to Denmark Vesey's Bible study in Charleston, from the unnamed griot's circle in the brush arbors to Sojourner Truth's prayers with her mother in the woods of New York, enslaved African Americans heard a clear, prophetic word in the gospel of Jesus—namely, freedom. Yet their assertion of this truth was met with condescension, rebuke, and brutal attacks on their bodies. In 1822, when Denmark Vesey, who had purchased his own freedom, heard a call like that heard by Samson before him to fight for his people's liberation, he wasn't only executed for his interpretation of Scripture, his church, the Emanuel African Methodist Episcopal Church, also known as Mother Emanuel, was also burned down. Fort Sumter, where the first shots of the Civil War were fired, was rebuilt in Charleston's harbor, coincidentally, with one of its guns facing the rebuilt Mother Emanuel Church. While many white Christians forget this history, Dylann Roof did not. His terrorist attack on Mother Emanuel in 2015 was, as he said, designed to "start a race war." He hoped to pick up where nineteenth-century Christians had left off.

The overt and brutal violence of our segregated past and present reveal a much quieter violence that white Christians learned to live with in the nineteenth century. In the 1780s, after Quakers had abolished slavery in Pennsylvania, the formerly enslaved Richard Allen was ordained to preach the gospel at Saint George's Methodist Episcopal Church in Philadelphia. Allen's conviction was rooted in his personal experience of the gospel's power—and not only at Saint George's. Hearing Allen's testimony, his master had been moved to sign papers granting Allen freedom. After ordaining him, however, the white leadership of Saint George's consigned Allen to an early service, where fellow African Americans gathered to hear the good news. Perceived as a threat, Allen's congregation was soon barred from the building. No brutal attacks, just the raw use of power to subvert the gospel.

Allen did not back down. He led a nonviolent "pray-in" at Saint George's, and when he and his congregation were forcibly removed, he sued for the right to establish the African Methodist Episcopal church. While the AME is widely celebrated as the first black church in America, it's important to note that it was founded not as a tribute to African American cultural pride but as a protest against white supremacy in the church. The AME wasn't a black church. It was a gospel church, prophetically calling out the quiet violence of every denomination that did not embrace the full membership of its African American sisters and brothers.

Over the next generation, as America's original sin led the nation ever closer to a civil war that would separate North from South, Christians anticipated the division by the fracturing of their denominational bodies. In 1838, Presbyterians split over the question of slavery. Methodist Episcopalians followed in 1844, and the Baptists, officially, in 1845. Long before the body politic was ripped in two, the body of Christ was broken by the quiet violence of white supremacy.

When the war was over and African American Christians gained citizenship in the South, their white Christian neighbors did not repent and ask forgiveness for their sins. Visit historic black churches throughout the South today, and you'll find cornerstones marked 1865. With the legal right to own property, formerly enslaved Christians followed Richard Allen and others before them to establish congregations where the Christianity of the slaveholder did not hold sway. Today, we call these congregations "black churches" and often assume that people self-segregate because of cultural differences that are value neutral. But our racial habits are directly connected to a violent and heretical past. A gospel that does not interrupt them perpetuates a church that is broken by sin.

A Dangerous Redemption

Many well-meaning efforts at racial reconciliation today gloss over the fact of the American church's broken body and the ways its wounds have been passed down to us through racial habits. This isn't only true among us Christians who have learned to think of ourselves as white. Asian Americans, Latinos, Native Americans, and African Americans are often invited to proclaim and practice a gospel that glosses over the realities of our shared history and the practices of the present.

We are all subject to the lie of slaveholder religion and the ways it has continued to reassert itself. But to see how racial habits are written into our religious cultures—to really grasp how the circle on Ms. Carolyn's porch offers a model for the body of Christ—we need to pay closer attention to what happened among Christians after America's Civil War during Reconstruction.

"The Battle Hymn of the Republic" remains in Christian hymnals as a reminder that, as President Lincoln preached during the Civil War, the concern of the Union was "to be on God's side, for God is always right." While many in the North thanked God for victory, celebrating the vindication of their righteous cause, and formerly enslaved people marked 1865 as their year of Jubilee, the broken body of Christ in America did not return to full communion. Within the body politic, Reconstruction emerged as the official effort to reunify the nation and guarantee full citizenship to people who had been legally held in bondage. But within American Christianity, a continuation of racial segregation was sanctioned as Redemption.

To understand the postwar conversations in churches, we have to remember what was happening in politics. The United States had been constituted on a compromise among white men that could no longer hold after nearly a century—namely, that Southern plantation owners could have three-fifths of the political power that came from counting enslaved people toward democratic representation without acknowledging those people as citizens. As late as 1857, the Supreme Court had ruled in its Dred Scott decision that not only enslaved people but all of their descendants—that is, anyone seen as black in America—were "so far inferior that they had no rights which the white man was bound to respect." This was the respectable and legal arrangement that Bishop Freeman and Rev. Stringfellow, along with millions of other white Christians, had used Scripture to justify until and throughout the Civil War.

But federal Reconstruction meant something incredibly important for American Christianity: for the first time, a significant number of black preachers throughout the South proclaimed the gospel in the public square. When they did, the God who had raised Israel out of Egypt before raising Jesus from the dead cried out and spared not, in the tradition of the ancient prophets. Yes, Jesus offered personal salvation to each and every person who would repent of their sins and follow him. A battalion of preachers saw political engagement as a necessary task of pastoral vocation, on the basic tenets that would be written into the Thirteenth, Fourteenth, and Fifteenth Amendments to the Constitution, the Reconstruction Amendments: the abolition of slavery, equal citizenship and equal protection under the law, and equal access to voting. The lay preacher Frederick Douglass summed up their prophetic cry: "Slavery is not abolished until the black man has the ballot." White Christians did not rush to the altar to embrace this good news. It took another five years of political struggle after the bloody end of the Civil War for the US Congress to ratify the Fifteenth Amendment. Douglass's adage once again summed up the reality that "power concedes nothing without a demand."

But as evidenced in the massacre at the Colfax Courthouse five years later, many white Christians hardly conceded to the demands of black citizenship. Instead, their preachers warned against the dangers of "Negro rule" and corrupt carpetbaggers, eager to make a dollar off the South's misfortune. These preachers decried the political religionism of their colleagues who came South with missionary zeal to join hands with black preachers and proclaim the gospel of equality. This was not a Reconstruction of the American republic, they insisted. It was, instead, a tragic era of immorality. Such rhetoric sanctioned a rejection of base-level racial reconciliation in public life by any means necessary. Not everyone was comfortable with the crude violence of Christian terrorist organizations such as the Ku Klux Klan and the Red Shirts, another white-supremacist paramilitary group active after the Civil War. But they were hardly condemned; the crusade against black citizenship, like race-based slavery before it, had won theological justification as "redemption."

Growing up in Shelby, North Carolina, during this period, Rev. Thomas Dixon Jr. inherited the Redemption movement's biblical imagination for white supremacy. Studying at Johns Hopkins, he befriended Woodrow Wilson before going on to serve pulpits in North Carolina, Boston, and New York City. By the turn of the century, Rev. Dixon was beginning to be recognized as the nation's greatest preacher—the Billy Graham of America's pre-television era. National exposure helped Rev. Dixon experience how much of the rest of the country looked down on his native South. Never one to lack for words, he set out to correct this popular view of white Southerners with a series of popular novels.

Dixon's second book, *The Clansman*, was certainly not the first attempt to paint Redemption in a positive light. But millions of Americans would never have internalized the narrative of Dixon's fiction if D. W. Griffith had not turned *The Clansman* into one of cinema's first feature films, *The Birth of a Nation*. By the time it debuted in 1915, Rev. Dixon's college buddy, Woodrow Wilson, had left his post as president of Princeton University to serve as president of the United States. To celebrate Dixon's success, Wilson hosted the first screening of a motion picture in the White House, giving this passionate defense of Redemption a national platform. The Ku Klux Klan had the president to thank for its most effective recruiting tool in the early twentieth century.

As terrifying as this history may be to twenty-first-century Christians looking back, we cannot ignore the fact that it is our history. Dixon's propaganda cannot be dismissed as lies from the secular media or corrupt politicians. *The Birth of a Nation* is Christian propaganda, written and popularized by a Baptist preacher who went on to start one of New York City's first non-denominational churches. When *The Clansman* was reviewed by *The Biblical Recorder* in North Carolina, the preachers who baptized my grandparents were encouraged to see their fathers and grandfathers reimagined as an

> Invisible Empire of defeated soldiers who in poverty and weakness by the might of right and courage of consecration to all that is holy, terrorized the aliens that had assumed to rule them, disarmed the black cohorts, struck down their white satraps, and drove out from the Temple of our Liberties the horde that had been put in possession of the holy of holies itself.

These were men they had known—loved ones they had buried in the graveyards behind their churches. But the myths that glorified their Confederate dead depended on church communities divided by race—a broken body of Christ where the grandparents of sisters and brothers at the AME Zion congregation or "the other First Baptist" in every Southern town could be dismissed as "black cohorts," and never remembered as loved ones whose stories had hardly been told.

Worshiping in Spirit and in Truth

Our history as it was experienced by people labeled non-white has hardly been told by them in our history books, on the big screen, or from prominent pulpits. But it was passed down, one generation to the next, on porches like Ms. Carolyn's. Whenever that circle of trust has existed—wherever people who have been *raced* as other have gathered to stay sane and make sense of their world—the gospel of Jesus has connected with power.

This was as true in first-century Palestine as it is in America today, which is why Jesus was celebrated by migrant field workers, nonunionized longshoremen, the sick and the lame, the despised and rejected. Wherever these people gathered, the message of Jesus was received as a word of life. But when Jesus confronted the political establishment, the religious authorities, and the corporate masters in their spaces of power, our gentle Savior tended to cause a ruckus.

At the synagogue in his hometown, the locals took Jesus outside and tried to throw him off a cliff. At the temple in Jerusalem, he got into a fight with local businessmen. Preachers from all the major denominations of his day trolled Jesus, asking gotcha questions whenever he was addressing a crowd. He tried open-air revival meetings, but they eventually got him killed.

If Jesus came to start the church, he didn't have much success in what we think of as typical church meetings. (Though some of his one-liners to the hecklers are great. Jesus could have done well on Twitter.) Still, Jesus connected with everyday people and invited them into God's movement on the porches of his day.

One of those circles of trust was a well in Samaria. John's Gospel makes clear that Jesus wasn't supposed to be there. A Jew walking through Samaria then was something like a middle-class white couple strolling through a historically black neighborhood in America today. If that same couple were invited up onto a neighbor's porch to sit down and hear the stories of the place—well, that would be something like the social setting of a Jew sitting down with the Samaritan woman. John tells us this is what Jesus did.

The Samaritan woman knew Jesus wasn't supposed to be on her porch, but she wasn't much worried about his social transgression. She wanted to talk about the beef between Jews and Samaritans. And she knew it was rooted in religion. As we say on Ms. Carolyn's porch, this sister was "keepin' it real."

"Well, tell me this: Our ancestors worshiped God at this mountain, but you Jews insist that Jerusalem is the only place for worship, right?" she seems to say.

This Samaritan woman isn't a history major. She's not lecturing Jesus about religious differences she has studied. She's asking about the racial habits that were passed down to her by everyone who ever sat around this well that their father Jacob dug, passing down stories that told them who they were.

Jesus offers the only response that can heal the broken body of God's family in the world. Jesus sits with the Samaritan woman on her porch. He joins her in her place, swapping stories. Not a big thing in one sense. Just two people together, talking.

But Jesus says this is enough to alter the course of history: "The time is coming—it has, in fact, come—when what you're called will not matter and where you go to worship will not matter." Before this woman has believed anything new or prayed a prayer—before Jesus' death and resurrection—a history of religious division is healed because bodies that have been segregated are sitting together. On a porch.

The church is broken by slaveholder religion. We bear the wound in our bodies, and we witness it in the racial habits of Christ's body, broken. But Jesus says a time is coming—it has, in fact, long since come—when we will worship God in spirit and in truth by crossing the racial divide in American Christianity and sitting down with sisters and brothers who already know Jesus for themselves. Wherever this happens, the kingdom of God is already close enough to touch.

In the summer of 1964, when America faced the challenge of Reconstruction for a second time during the civil rights movement, hundreds of young people—black and white— traveled south to Mississippi. Freedom Summer was a nonviolent troop surge designed to heighten the moral crisis of Jim Crow disenfranchisement. One hundred years after the Fifteenth Amendment had guaranteed them the ballot, African Americans still just wanted to participate in American democracy. It was a long, hot summer in which many people's faith was tested and three young men lost their lives. Through the organization of the new, multiethnic Mississippi Freedom Democratic Party, the movement took its challenge all the way to the Democratic National Convention in Atlantic City, New Jersey. Though they weren't seated that summer, they changed the conversation in American politics, and the Voting Rights Act, prohibiting racial discrimination in voting, became law the next year.

But for many students from Northern universities, the experience of Freedom Summer that had the longest-lasting impact was sitting on front porches by dirt roads in rural Mississippi, listening to stories and being welcomed into "beloved community." Even if they didn't call it church, they were testifying to the gospel. What happened on those porches may not have changed everything, but it changed them, inspiring a generation of community builders.

6

A GILDED CROSS IN THE PUBLIC SQUARE

★

*C*hange *your racial habits* and you change the way you see the world.

It doesn't happen all at once. When you open your eyes after a lifetime of blindness, the light can be unbearable. Real conversion takes time. Maybe you see people, but they "look like trees walking around" (Mark 8:24). Without a doubt, there are many details and nuances you cannot see at all. But as you change your habits, you begin to meet new people and hear new stories—not just on a page or screen but living in bodies like yours, people you know and may even come to love. No, it doesn't happen all at once, but every day these new experiences are laying new neural pathways in your mind. Follow where they lead, and you start to realize you're getting born again.

For me, Ms. Carolyn's porch became a portal to another city, one that existed alongside the only Durham I'd ever known, like a parallel universe. A thousand conversations and invitations led me from that porch to a new community—dinner at Chicken Hut and lunch-to-go from the back of a gas station. I got to know barbershops and liquor houses, birthday parties in jazz clubs, and family reunions on the Fourth of July at cousin Joe's place out in the country. In this universe, I met Nora's cousin, who was an electrician on the side; and brother Joseph, who knew plumbing; Keisha's boyfriend, who could work on your car out in the driveway late at night; and Mr. Bell, who kept everything you needed for a neighborhood block party under his house in the crawl space. Ms. Aubura ran a daycare out of her living room. Ms. Dot, in her nineties, had been porch sitting longer than anyone. If you couldn't find what you needed anywhere else, you could ask her.

Here was a wealth of wisdom and community that I'd been cut off from—one I hadn't even known I was missing, imagining myself to be a capable, educated middle-class individual. One of the illusions of whiteness, I'd begun to realize, was that each of us is somehow a world unto ourselves, responsible for the choices we make and the relationships we choose.

But the compound effect of sin-sick individuals is an unjust society. Along with racial blindness and racial habits, white people have inherited racial politics. Like our racial habits, racial politics have little to do with how each of us feels about other individuals. Try to talk to a white person about racial politics and the go-to response is some version of "that's not what my black friends say." And it's true—because racial politics has never been about hating the people you know. Racial politics is about dividing us from people we don't know through fear, then offering a savior to make us feel secure.

And righteous. In America, racial politics has always been "Christian"—has always cloaked itself in the language of redemption and morality. Co-opting the poor refugee Christ to defend white supremacy, we have crucified him on a gilded cross, turning the most revolutionary symbol of our movement into a talisman to finger when we're anxious. Meanwhile, the gold-plated illusions that the real Jesus died to free us from continue to be our frame of reference, however much we may lament its imperfections.

In all of this, we miss the basic message of the gospel and the wisdom of untold millions who've shown us a better way. "The stone the builders rejected / has become the cornerstone" (Psalm 118:22).

The Wisdom of Rejected Stones

In the new world to which I was welcomed from Ms. Carolyn's porch, one person kept showing up, over and again. Everyone called her Ms. Ann, and I could tell from the way folks said her name that she was a force. Fifty years earlier, Ann Atwater had been a single mother, living in Hayti, the heart of Durham's African American community. When a local organizer recognized her capacity to reach everyday people, she was recruited to attend a sixteen-week Community Action Training, then went to work as a community organizer. "Pretty soon I was kicking butt and taking names," she later said. Ms. Ann became sergeant of the local foot soldiers in Durham's civil rights movement.

In 1971, the federal government sent in a mediator to facilitate the desegregation of Durham's public schools (an action the Supreme Court had ordered seventeen years earlier "with all deliberate speed"). In a surprising move, the federal agent invited Ann Atwater to cochair the process with her arch nemesis, C. P. Ellis, a local leader in the Ku Klux Klan. "Hell, no!" she reportedly told the mediator. But soon she realized that, without her participation, the Klan would have sole control of the process. "I called him back and said, 'I'd be happy to serve as cochair,'" Ann later recalled. Thus the desegregation of Durham's schools was cooled by an avowed white supremacist and a militant black activist.

Over the course of their meetings, C. P. and Ann learned some things about each other. Both of their families were poor, and poor kids weren't being served well by public schools, no matter the color of their skin. History and political powers pitted black and white against each other, but when self-interest compelled C. P. and Ann to work together, they came to see how much they had in common. At the end of their public meetings, C. P. tore up his Klan card and Ann embraced him as a brother.

This was the Ms. Ann whom folks in Durham still called on when they needed something from the powers that be. Walking through the doorways that opened up from Ms. Carolyn's porch and a dozen other spaces that weren't controlled by the norms of whiteness, I'd begun to realize that I needed something from Ms. Ann too. I wasn't quite sure how to name it, but I felt a basic contradiction between my experience of community on Ms. Carolyn's porch and the ways I could imagine trying to change the world.

Everything I knew about race taught me to think that I was white while Ms. Ann and Ms. Carolyn were black. Everything I knew about faith taught me that Jesus loved me and I could love him back by loving my neighbors as myself. But in the segregated worlds that whiteness had created, I'd inherited a false sense of superiority that suggested Christian charity meant white people helping black people. Fellow pale-skinned Christians who saw me crossing the color line in Durham shared this assumption—and responded awkwardly whenever I questioned it. "I don't hang out on my neighbor's porch for her sake," I told white friends, trying to be honest. "I'm learning to porch sit for my sake"—which was true. But I was also learning on that porch that my decisions weren't just about me.

There are, in fact, huge disparities that point to systemic injustice in twenty-first-century America. From lack of access to education and job opportunities to the disparate impacts of disease and incarceration, black bodies in America continue to bear an unfair share of humanity's burden. To do nothing, even in protest of my white privilege, is itself an injustice. If his neighbor were hungry, Jesus would feed her. If there were policies that made it harder for people to feed themselves, Jesus would challenge them.

But how? How do Christians faithfully engage the societies in which we live—especially after we've realized how race has warped our vision of the world and of ourselves? For far too long, racial politics kept me from the wisdom of Ann Atwater and the black-led freedom movement she represented. Like most people formed by whiteness, I thought you read a book or went to school to learn how to engage the world. While faith might inspire us to love our neighbor, the experts and the politicians would tell us how to put together the building blocks of a healthy society.

Racial politics keeps us from seeing that the gospel turns these assumptions on their head. If Jesus Christ is risen from the dead, then the stone that society's experts rejected is the key to the success of our common life. I needed to learn a new kind of politics, and Ann Atwater was the teacher God gave me.

I drove over to Ms. Ann's house and tried to explain what I needed. "I spent a lot of time in school," I told her, "but I never learned what you know."

"Well, what I do is pretty simple," she said.

"Okay," I said, "tell me how you do it."

"I listen to you until I understand what you want, then I help you get it. And when we get about halfway to what you want, I tell you what I want."

She smiled, satisfied with the simplicity of her description. Ms. Ann was not naive. She had been involved in Durham's public life for half a century and was widely recognized as a local hero. Schools and housing developments had been named after her, books and plays chronicled her story, and she lectured regularly at colleges and universities. But she lived in the same Department of Housing and Urban Development (HUD) housing and did the same organizing work she'd been recruited to do half a century earlier because she was good at it.

Ann's politics didn't ignore self-interest, but she obviously wasn't self-serving either. She described a way of life she had practiced—a way that was practical, however unlikely it might seem. She had shared her story and experience with thousands of people, but she didn't pretend to be an expert. She was passing on to me what others had passed on to her. It was as simple as that—with one catch. She knew her wisdom wasn't a set of theoretical ideas that I could memorize and take with me. It was, instead, a living tradition.

"I'll teach you everything I know," Ms. Ann told me, "but you've got to do one thing. You got to become my son."

I agreed to the deal, and I became part of a family that exposed the lie of racial politics. When Leah and I completed the required classes to adopt our oldest son, Grandma Ann was there for our graduation ceremony. Throughout America's Obama years, our kids grew up listening to her commentary on the world. Grandma Ann gave us what she had given C. P. Ellis— what she freely offered anyone who wanted it. She gave us an identity that ran deeper than the racial politics of black and white. Grandma Ann loved us into her freedom family, and in doing so showed us how the way of Jesus contradicts the basic patterns of the world that white supremacy built.

The World White Supremacy Built

When she moved to Durham from rural Columbus County, Grandma Ann was following a young man she had married. He had promised to go ahead of her and the child they were expecting to prepare a home. When she received an address where she could find him, she didn't know it was for a boarding house where he was sharing a room with a man neither of them knew. At her insistence, Ann and her husband rented their own place for a little while, but by the time he left her, their first baby girl had been born and another was on the way. Grandma Ann found work as a domestic, cleaning white women's houses, and scrambled to raise two girls on her own.

Grandma Ann learned from experience the political and economic system that Zora Neale Hurston summed up so well in *Their Eyes Were Watching God*.

Honey, de white man is de ruler of everything as fur as Ah been able tuh find out. Maybe it's some place way off in de ocean where de black man is in power, but we don't know nothin' but what we see. So de white man throw down de load and tell de nigger man tuh pick it up. He pick it up because he have to, but he don't tote it. He hand it to his womenfolks. De nigger woman is de mule uh de world so fur as Ah can see.

Given the burden she bore as a mule of the world, Grandma Ann could have easily hated the white man who inherited power by default, the white woman who assumed she was superior, or the black man who left her when he couldn't take the pressure anymore. Carrying the weight of a whole society on her back, she could have resented the Mexican immigrant who seemed to find work more easily than she did or the sister who stole her man. She might have despaired, giving up hope all together.

But she didn't. Instead, Grandma Ann learned to see through the pitfalls of racial politics to confront a system that made everyone less than God had created them to be. Grandma Ann knew that injustice was unnatural. People—not God—had set up this system. People were going to have to come together to fix it.

Grandma Ann was a veteran of America's most celebrated effort to confront systemic racism—the twentieth century's civil rights movement. The political achievements of her lifetime were real, and they echoed the demands of America's First Reconstruction: the abolition of slavery, full citizenship in public life and equal protection under the law, and equal access to the ballot. What the Thirteenth, Fourteenth, and Fifteenth Amendments had not in fact secured for African Americans, Grandma Ann and many others had worked to guarantee through direct action to desegregate public accommodations and political organizing to pass the Civil Rights Act of 1964, the Voting Rights Act of 1965, and the Fair Housing Act of 1968.

Grandma Ann organized for systemic change because Jesus called her to love her neighbor as herself. But she knew well that neither black nor white churches in her lifetime had universally embraced a prophetic challenge of the world that white supremacy built. Stokely Carmichael coined the term "institutional racism" in his 1967 book *Black Power*, summing up what Grandma Ann's generation had learned from experience: *people have to change the unjust systems that people built.* But forty years later, the basic notion that economic and political systems function to exclude people of color from access to power was still offensive to many Christians. Indeed, faith seemed to create an internal resistance to systemic change.

Whenever church folks talked to Grandma Ann, she wanted to talk about how public schools continued to fail poor students—how they were resegregating as a school-to-prison pipeline, guaranteeing that one in three African American boys born after 2000 would experience incarceration. She wanted to organize people of faith to challenge institutional racism.

But church folks almost always wanted to talk about how she had befriended a Klansman. People cried when they heard Grandma Ann's story. Overwhelmed by feelings of guilt, they confessed terrible things they had heard their parents say about black people behind closed doors. They apologized for not doing more to resist hatred and bigotry.

But I don't think I ever heard a single church person ask Grandma Ann who they should vote for in the next school-board election. Somehow, a faith that moved people to believe in racial reconciliation did not raise the issue of racial politics.

This wasn't a personal fault of individuals who sincerely lamented the sins of America's past. It was, instead, a persistent symptom of the world that white supremacy had built. A century earlier, faith leaders who supported the full citizenship of freed people in the South had been branded advocates of "political religionism." Preachers who defended Reconstruction were labeled "too political" by those who backed Redemption, no less political a movement. But once fear of black political power had been exploited to reinforce white supremacy in government, politicians called for peace and preachers encouraged Americans not to dwell on the past but to focus on the work of rebuilding. The book of Nehemiah, depicting the rebuilding of the walls of Jerusalem, became a favorite text among Southern preachers. Now that black political power had been checked, the very people who had decried Reconstruction started preaching about the virtues of rebuilding.

But this nation-building program extended far beyond the South. The Supreme Court's *Plessy v. Fergusson* decision, which offered legal precedent for "separate but equal," made clear by the end of the nineteenth century that America had preserved its Union without healing its racial politics. This was America at the dawn of the "Christian Century," on its way to world superpower status. Jim Crow's segregation was not an anomaly but a regional expression of the separate and unequal opportunities African Americans found in cities of the North and Midwest when they fled the terror of Southern lynching. This Great Migration was the largest internal displacement of people in US history, but after half a century, when Dr. Martin Luther King Jr. led an integrated march into Chicago's all-white suburbs in 1966, he said he witnessed hatred there he had never seen in Alabama or Mississippi. This from the man who just three years earlier had preached the funeral for four little girls in Birmingham who were dynamited by the Klan.

No, the world that white supremacy built wasn't confined to the South, and it had not gone away after Reconstruction. It had morphed and changed, impacting the lives of billions as America came to dominate the world stage. No one knew better than a black woman in Grandma Ann's position how little freedom meant in mid-twentieth-century America.

But the world that white supremacy built could not hear Grandma Ann's voice. And a faith that tried to practice Christian charity without confronting systemic injustice only reinforced this systematic silencing of Grandma Ann. Thank God she wouldn't be quiet. She often said, "God gave me a big mouth, so I used it to holler." A persistent woman, Grandma Ann helped me to see the virtue of stubbornness, which Jesus affirmed, even if American Christianity did not.

The Gift of Persistence

While most Christians today recognize Dr. Martin Luther King Jr. as both a great American and a great preacher, he was not affirmed by a majority of Christians in his own day, black or white. Southern white segregationists, of course, dismissed King as Martin Luther Coon. It's easy today to conjure an image of a Klan preacher spewing hatred against the civil rights movement at a rally around a fiery cross. But while such preaching did exist, it was certainly not the only Christianity to oppose King's effort to expose and transform racial politics in America. Dr. King's own denomination, the National Baptist Convention, pushed him out, along with other Baptist preachers who insisted on confronting the world white supremacy had built. King's "Letter from Birmingham Jail," perhaps his most famous written work, was written in response to seven Christian ministers and a rabbi in Alabama. Though high school and college students study King's letter as a primary document in twentieth-century American history, the theological reasoning he was responding to gets little attention. Christians in American would do well to study the ministers' joint letter in our Sunday schools; in so many ways, it sums up our habit of resisting challenges to America's racial politics.

In the opening lines of their "Good Friday Statement," sent to Dr. King April 12, 1963, the ministers note that they have already written "An Appeal for Law and Order and Common Sense," a statement sent to him January 16, 1963. They do not try to defend the world that white supremacy built. In fact, they had acknowledged the existence of "various problems which cause racial friction and unrest." But they object firmly to the way in which Dr. King and the civil rights movement had been confronting Jim Crow laws, demanding change through nonviolent direct action. However just the cause, they insist, it "should be pressed in the courts and in negotiations among local leaders, and not in the streets."

Such was the "Common Sense" of most Christians in 1960s Birmingham. Realists in the tradition of theologians like Reinhold Niebuhr, these Alabama clergy understood the messiness of politics and the necessity of engaging immoral society for the sake of social change. But they thought they understood how change must be pursued: legally, and with deference to the order that white supremacy built and Bull Connor controlled. Anything else, however peaceful it might seem, contributed to hatred and violence in their assessment.

Dr. King objected, and his polemical response is what we remember half a century later. But the fact that the ecumenical leadership of the faith community in Alabama at the time felt self-assured in making this statement is a testimony to how prevalent their political realism was across theological traditions.

In mid-twentieth-century Alabama, as is often the case today, the religious leadership of American Christianity had more in common with the Pharisees and Sadducees of first-century Jerusalem than with the movement of Jesus. In the Gospel accounts of Jesus' crucifixion, the Roman authorities arrest Jesus, but they are ready to release him after examination. "I find no basis for a charge against this man," said Pilate, the chief law enforcement officer in Jerusalem. But the crowd and religious leaders insist, "Crucify him!" (Luke 23:4, 20). The religious leaders, even more than the secular, insist that "law and order" must crucify our Lord.

Why were a Roman proconsul in the first century and the Supreme Court in the twentieth century quicker than the local religious leadership to side with the way of Jesus? For the Gospel writers, this question is at the heart of what it means to receive the message of Jesus.

All four Gospels record a version of a story about a persistent woman who insisted on anointing Jesus before he went to Jerusalem to face the systems of his day and suffer their most extreme punishment. In Luke's account, she interrupts the rare dinner that Jesus ate with religious leaders to wash his feet with her tears, dry them with her hair, and anoint his feet with an expensive perfume.

Her act of devotion is offensive on several levels to the Pharisee who is hosting Jesus. Socially, men in first-century Palestine took their meals separately from women. Her presence among men interrupted the social order of Jesus' day. But her transgression moves quickly beyond the socially unacceptable to the immoral. "If this man were a prophet," Jesus' host says of him, "he would know who is touching him and what kind of woman she is—that she is a sinner" (Luke 7:39).

Like Dr. King two thousand years later, Jesus is numbered with the transgressors. However good his intentions, he is associating with the wrong people and going about things the wrong way. But the Gospel writers are clear: this persistent woman who insists on anointing Jesus sees something that the religious leadership has missed—Jesus is the king of the universe.

It's no accident that this anointing is prelude to Jesus' civil disobedience in Jerusalem in all four Gospels. No doubt this persistent woman is crossing social and moral lines when she pours fragrant oil over the feet of Jesus. But she is also engaging in an explicitly political act. In ancient Israel, kings were set apart as political leaders of God's people through ritual anointing. In America's democracy, we affirm the election of presidents with an inauguration that culminates in the oath of office. In the Bible, kings don't take an oath; they are anointed. Jesus rides into Jerusalem in an inaugural parade to the adulation of adoring crowds because others believe, as this persistent woman did, that Jesus is King, the Messiah. To worship him is to celebrate the justice of a whole new political system.

This is why, in Mark's Gospel, the story of this persistent woman anointing Jesus ends with these words from Jesus himself: "Wherever the gospel is preached throughout the world, what she has done will also be told" (Mark 14:9). There is no way to preach the gospel without proclaiming that the unjust systems of this world must give way to the reign of a new King.

Just such political religion landed Jesus on the cross, and it is little surprise that religious leaders who have accommodated themselves to the world that white supremacy built would adopt crosses of their own to kill movements that challenge that system. But as in the Gospel stories, persistent women continue to cross dividing lines to worship the God who saves us from racial politics.

For me, her name was Ann Atwater. She adopted me as her own, ignoring the social and moral boundaries of the South she grew up in. But that was not all. She also insisted that I know King Jesus—the Lord for whom friendship is always political because we live in a world where friends get hurt by injustice. To be a disciple of Jesus and a son of Ann Atwater, she told me, is to be in a quarrel with the world. Yes, our greatest weapon is love. But when we love in public, it looks like a disruption. Wherever I preach the gospel, Grandma Ann's disruption of America's racial politics must be told.

Part II

THE
CHRISTIANITY
OF CHRIST

7

THE OTHER HALF
OF HISTORY

★

In the eyes of white people who had been blinded by race, the black political power represented by the Colfax Courthouse in 1873 was a desecration of everything they believed to be sacred. Their Easter Sunday massacre captures in a single scene how slaveholder religion ultimately turns the gospel against itself, crucifying the black flesh of Christ's body in America.

But for those with eyes to see—for an American church not held captive by racial blindness, racial habits, and racial politics—the site of the Colfax massacre is holy ground. The men who were martyred there believed in the possibility of a new world that radically disrupted the political and religious leadership of their day. Their faith in equality didn't simply look forward to the sweet by and by but stood firmly on the solid ground of God's Word in the here and now. It reached back to the promises whispered to them during slavery, like the religious instruction Sojourner Truth's mother had given to her as a small child:

"My children, there is a God who hears and sees you."

"A God, mau-mau! Where does he live?" asked the children.

"He lives in the sky," she replied, "and when you are beaten or cruelly treated, or fall into any trouble, you must ask help of him, and he will always hear and help you."

Like the Hebrew children under Egypt's bondage, enslaved Christians in America cried out to God in heaven for salvation from their hell on earth. "I got shoes, you got shoes / all God's children got shoes," they sang, confessing a faith in things hoped for, despite evidence of shoes not seen. Still, their faith offered moral clarity as they named in song the hypocrisy of the slaveholder's religion: "Everybody talkin' 'bout heaven ain't goin' there."

Prophetic fire pressed faith to act, transforming spirituals sung during worship into invitations to escape. "I prayed for freedom for twenty years," Frederick Douglass would later write, "but received no answer until I prayed with my legs." For Douglass, the slaveholders' careful distinctions between body and soul meant little. If the gospel was good news, then it meant freedom from bondage.

What mattered for evangelical abolitionists in the nineteenth century was the emergence of a new society in the midst of the old that no longer believed or practiced the lie of slavery. From the Cane Ridge Revival in Kentucky in 1801 on through the 1850s at the peak of the Second Great Awakening, which gave rise to Baptist and Methodist churches across the South, the experience of conversion and worship across dividing lines compelled women and men to question their assumptions about race. These interruptions met resistance, both in the hearts of individual slaveholders and in the legislatures of slaveholding states. But a new community of white evangelicals and black freedmen, Quakers and enslaved people emerged, connecting souls across the unquestionable lines race had drawn on their bodies. Sisters and brothers in Christ, they became aliens in a strange land, without any clear pathway toward a country where they might live as equals. Still, they worked to establish a new community that, however imperfect, strove to live the ethic of God's kingdom in nineteenth-century America.

After Frederick Douglass had "prayed with his legs," he connected with pale-skinned people across the Atlantic who helped purchase his freedom and with William Lloyd Garrison, a white evangelical who burned with a passion for Jesus and justice as editor of *The Liberator*, the nation's largest abolitionist newspaper. As Sarah Grimké emerged from her racial blindness as the daughter of a slaveholder in South Carolina, she discovered a new community in the network of people, homes, and periodicals that made up the Underground Railroad. Hundreds of lesser-known women and men, grounded in the Christianity of Christ, fleshed out small and imperfect pockets of freedom even as they worked tirelessly for the abolition that they knew would come eventually, even if not in their lifetime.

This is not to say that they didn't have their doubts. In a famous scene at Boston's Faneuil Hall, Frederick Douglass despaired in a talk to fellow abolitionists, airing his doubts that the slaveholder caucus in Congress would ever relent in their struggle to hold onto human property. Rising from her seat, Sojourner Truth reportedly shouted, "Frederick, is God dead?" Inscribed on her gravestone, these words are a testament to the faith that was passed down to one of the nineteenth century's greatest evangelists and shared with a movement of people, black and white, who trusted the way of Jesus over and against the established Christianity of their land.

We cannot see clearly what compelled those freedom fighters who defied state and federal law to do what they knew was right without contemplating the prayers and hopes of millions of people who understood the Emancipation Proclamation as a declaration of God's Jubilee. To them, Abraham Lincoln's assassination on Good Friday 1865 was a crucifixion that called forth the resurrection of a new political order in Reconstruction. This new America, both prefigured and practiced in the interracial coalitions of the abolition movement, was an expression of a peculiar people's faith. In his monumental history of this period, *Black Reconstruction*, W. E. B. DuBois noted simply, "God was real. They knew him."

But if God had, in the words of James Weldon Johnson, brought them "over a way that with tears has been watered . . . treading our path through the blood of the slaughtered," then the one who had been faithful through every generation did not abandon his children when the federal government gave up Reconstruction. Just as the faith of the Pharisees had morphed through the centuries to prop up the Christianity of the slaveholder and fuel the fire of the Klan, so too did the Christianity of Christ find places to flourish, however stony the ground of the American story.

More than 150 years later, we are all, to some degree at least, inheritors of both traditions. There is nowhere you can go to find the pure, peaceable, and unadulterated Christianity of Christ. The slaveholder religion has infected us all. But that is not to say that all forms of faith are created equal. However imperfectly, the disciples of Jesus passed on to the generation after them what had been passed down to them. Through twists and turns, the message of the gospel inspired the women and men who trusted that Reconstruction was possible, even as it was brutally attacked by fellow Christians. Their movement—America's black-led freedom movement—passed down to one generation after another a faith that had been whispered and hummed along the routes of the Underground Railroad.

In the story of American Christianity, it would be hard to imagine an inheritance more precious than this tradition. Yet, for most of American history and in most of America's churches, little has been done to preserve, honor, and pass on this faith of the black-led freedom movement.

From the other side of history, the site of the Colfax massacre, and dozens of forgotten places like it, is holy ground. When we take time to listen, the blood of martyrs cries out from this ground, inviting us to see, even now, that another way is always possible.

On Pilgrimage in America

Vincent Harding taught me to pay attention to the holy ground that we often forget in the American story. An African American colleague and colaborer of Dr. Martin Luther King Jr., Dr. Harding was also a historian who saw the world through the eyes of faith. He knew well the importance of memory for people's movements, but he wanted to build movements, not monuments. Dr. Harding believed, as Revelation reprises from Psalm 46, that "there is a river whose streams make glad the city of God" (Psalm 46:4). That great river flows through history, connecting people of faith to the Christianity of Christ. Dr. Harding's life's work was to baptize people into that river.

I met Dr. Harding after a friend in Birmingham, Alabama, called to ask if I would gather a busload of young people from the Southeast to come spend a few days with Dr. Harding, soaking in the memories of that place and considering together what the freedom movement looks like today. This was before Black Lives Matter, but young people in Walltown—much like young people of color elsewhere—were angry about racial profiling and the number of people who looked like them in our jail. We decided to make a 21st Century Freedom Ride together and to start with a public forum on racial profiling in our neighborhood. Every pilgrimage begins somewhere.

When God called Abram in Genesis 12, his destination was unclear. "Go from your country, your people and your father's household to the land I will show you" (Genesis 12:1). Abram did not know where he was going, but God's call focused Abram's attention on what he needed to leave behind: "your country, your people and your father's household." To begin to imagine ourselves on pilgrimage in America is to acknowledge, like the abolitionists before us, that we are aliens in a strange land. This world is not our home, and the nation we have known is not our true country. Not only was this land stolen from the indigenous people who were here before us, but also, in a broader sense, we have never yet been the land of the free and the home of the brave that we aspire to become. If we are honest, there is no time in our history we can return to when everything was as we say it should be.

In the most practical sense, the promise of an America with liberty and justice for all is something we must leave the country and people and households we've known to discover. To be true to our faith as well as our nation's aspirations is to be on pilgrimage.

Dr. Harding taught us that every pilgrimage toward freedom begins with attention to our basic identity. "Where did you spend your childhood?" he asked each person, even the ones who were still children. "And where did your maternal grandmother spend her childhood?" Each of us comes from a household and a story, Dr. Harding knew. "Tell me her name," he said, leaning forward with his gentle smile.

Before our freedom ride was done, "Uncle Vincent" had adopted us all, inviting us into the freedom family that stretched from the Hebrew midwives in ancient Egypt to the enslaved mothers of Southern plantations to "Ella's Song" in the twentieth century. "We who believe in freedom cannot rest" became our anthem. But our voices, though they could be joined in harmony, were not the same. We had to wrestle with the stories we'd heard at our grandmothers' knees—with the ways each of our fathers' households had taught us something about who our people are.

I watched young white people on that freedom ride unpack their so-called privilege, questioning basic assumptions about success and faithfulness. Our liberation was tied to that of young undocumented sisters and brothers who were also questioning the American dream—how the future it promised did not include their own parents. A formerly incarcerated African American man stood tall, celebrating a newfound pride that he was the son of women and men who had shown America what freedom means. An unlikely gang—black, white, and brown—went out in into a Birmingham neighborhood on break one afternoon and brought back a local elder with her own stories to tell about marching against Bull Connor's dogs fifty years earlier. We were, in fact, on holy ground, surrounded by saints we might have missed if we hadn't stopped to pay attention.

The other half of history doesn't erase everything we ever thought we knew about ourselves and our God, but it does invite us to see all things in a new light. As pilgrims in a strange land, we leave our people and place for a country as yet unknown in order to see and name the holy ground beneath our feet. This cannot be a solitary journey because it entails the sharing of very different and often painful stories. But in the people who bear those stories, we meet the beloved community that both prefigures and prepares us for the country we've not yet been. The other half of history is an invitation to live into another story.

Stepping into the River

Uncle Vincent helped me name the river of resistance and the way each of us as pilgrims can learn to see it where we are. But I met him because others had invited me to step into the river. We rarely find our way alone. Sammie helped me name my racial blindness, and Ms. Carolyn's porch opened my eyes to the racial habits that shaped my daily life. Grandma Ann showed us how to interrupt the racial politics of this place where we live. But I would never have met any of these important teachers—I wouldn't even have known I needed them—if it weren't for Rev. Barber.

After my stint in Strom Thurmond's office, I came back to North Carolina confused. I no longer believed in the fear-based politics that drove the religious right, but I didn't know what an alternative looked like. My Jesus was too white, but I didn't know where to go to learn how to read the Bible differently. I had a hunch that all was not right with the world I had inherited, but I was ignorant of the other half of history. I wasn't even a pilgrim, really—just a young man without a country.

A few months later, back home in North Carolina, I attended an event hosted by our governor's office. The keynote speaker for the evening was the state's human relations chair, an African American man named William J. Barber II. I didn't know he was a preacher when he stepped to the podium. But by the time he sat down, a ballroom full of people were on their feet, clapping and shouting like we were at a Pentecostal camp meeting. I was among them. Unsure of what had happened to us, I knew I had to hear more from Rev. Barber.

When I invited him to come preach at my home church, Rev. Barber graciously accepted. I met him in the parking lot and thanked him for coming. "I'm glad to be here," he said, "but I wasn't coming alone."

"Oh," I said, "you don't like to drive at night?"

"No, I know too many stories about what's happened to people who look like me up here," he said. Rev. Barber told me he wouldn't come to my hometown by himself because he knew its history. I was from Klan country.

Rev. Barber knew my history better than I did, and he knew the danger it presented to his body. But he still came. He told me I was an heir of America's racism, but he also told me I was his brother. If I was willing to turn from the lie that said people who looked like me knew how to run the world, Rev. Barber was ready to welcome me into America's freedom family—into the truest church that this land has ever known.

I didn't know then the fear he had to face to extend a hand to someone like me. I hadn't heard the stories he would later tell me about how, when his father was working for racial justice in Georgia, a white man had put a gun in his father's mouth and told him that if he didn't get out of town by morning, he wouldn't live to see the sun go down again. I didn't know about how, when Rev. Barber was a teenager, he had been watching TV at his uncle's house one evening when a burning cross lit up on the lawn outside. Rev. Barber's uncle handed him a shotgun and told him to stand at the back door and shoot anything that moved. These were the stories Rev. Barber carried in his body when he drove up to Klan country and extended a hand to me.

But they weren't the only stories he knew. Rev. Barber also knew the stories of people such as Clarence Jordan, Will Campbell, and Anne Braden—white Christians who had come to realize that the South's segregation didn't hurt only black people; it hurt them too. In the twentieth century these people had learned to follow the lead of freedom fighters such as Rosa Parks and Dr. King, stepping into a river of resistance that included black, white, and brown, rich and poor alike. Rev. Barber knew "there is a river," and he knew, by God's grace, that it even includes people who look like me. He extended a hand of welcome, and I began a journey into a world I would never have known without his gracious invitation.

Such hospitality is not uncommon in the history of America's black-led freedom movement. It's there in Richard Allen's insistence that the AME church was, from the beginning, not a church for black people but a church for *all* people. It's there in the cross-racial alliances of the Underground Railroad, in the white and black coalitions that came together in Southern statehouses during Reconstruction. It's there in the march across the Edmund Pettus Bridge in Selma, Alabama, which infuriated Sheriff Jim Clark all the more because the marchers were a mixed group. When millions of Americans witnessed "Bloody Sunday" in Selma on their TV in 1965, they saw law officers attacking unarmed citizens and heard Sheriff Clark shout: "Get those goddamned n------! And get those goddamned *white* n------!"

The most outrageous witness of the antiracist, black-led freedom movement in America has always been its radical insistence on the equality of all people. Those of us who hardly know the other half of history have a hard time even imagining this. Our racial blindness, it turns out, is our chief obstacle to receiving an invitation to join the beloved community. But when I was blind, Rev. Barber reached out and took me by the hand.

In John's Gospel, after Jesus has started a movement that challenged the power of the religious and political establishment, a man named Nicodemus came to visit Jesus under the cover of night. He came to Jesus, we can assume, because he had a hunch that there was room in Jesus' movement even for someone like him. But he came at night because he was part of the establishment. Nicodemus was like a white man.

Whiteness shines through the first words Nicodemus says to Jesus: "We know . . ." When the sick and the lame, the leprous and the outcast come to Jesus, they come saying, "Have mercy, Lord" and "if you are able, please . . ." But not Nicodemus. Here is a brother who has been brought up to assume that he understands how the world works and knows what is good and true. "We *know* that you are a teacher who has come from God" (John 3:2, emphasis added).

Like the rich young ruler who calls on him in the other Gospels—like everyone who ever comes to Jesus—our Lord looks at Nicodemus and loves him. But Jesus also knows that white men can't be saved until we face the fact that we do not know what we are doing. So Jesus tells Nicodemus, "You must be born again" (John 3:7).

This story, which was so central to white evangelicalism in the twentieth century, has been spiritualized to the point that it's nearly impossible to read afresh. And yet, as a white man who came to the black-led freedom movement under the cover of night, I can feel in my bones how much I need both the hospitality and the radical challenge of Jesus.

Jesus looked at this member of the Jewish ruling council—this young white man, just back from a stint in DC—and said something that Nicodemus—that I—could not even comprehend. "You must be born again."

When Nicodemus was born the first time, his mama and daddy had high hopes for him. They named him, in the king's English of the day (Greek), "victor of the people." Nicodemus was destined to be a hero. The world expected it of him, and he had learned to expect it of himself. No doubt, this is why Nicodemus is drawn to a popular teacher whom the local establishment has been talking about in its academic and religious circles. But Jesus is neither flattered nor put off. He sees through Nicodemus's mixed motives, and he sees precisely what he needs—namely, a new identity to live into.

"Born again," the Greek scholar and Southern agitator Clarence Jordan used to say, might be better translated "re-sired from above." That is, Jesus says to Nicodemus and every person ever born into America's so-called white privilege, "You aren't who your mama and daddy thought you were. You need to hear from heaven who you were made to be."

Jesus doesn't care what Nicodemus knows. Instead, he extends a hand of invitation—leave your people, your country, and your father's household and come be part of the beloved community.

I love how John's Gospel doesn't tell us what Nicodemus said in response or what he did that night. This story isn't about Nicodemus. It's not the story that's been told over and over about how, even when it comes to our original sin of race in America, white people have the answer. It's not about how Abraham Lincoln freed the slaves or Lyndon Johnson signed the Voting Rights Act or some white guy started a reconciliation ministry. No, John goes right on telling the story of Jesus' movement.

But Nicodemus isn't written out of the story. At the darkest moment, when Jesus' closest friends have betrayed him and the community he gathered together is in fragments, Nicodemus shows up to bury the body of the one who loved him to the end.

Yes, there is a place for everyone in the beloved community. But the "victor of the people" only finds his place—his true vocation—by learning to live a new politic among new friends, growing up into the new identity that has been offered from above.

8

MORAL REVIVAL

★

A man who knows he is blind doesn't pretend he can run on his own, much less pretend that he can lead others. But if someone with vision extends him a hand, he can begin to find his way.

The last thing any attempt to reconstruct the gospel in America needs is a white man to lead the charge. Yet, this is what whiteness conditions people like me and Nicodemus to imagine. If poverty is a problem, something inside of us wants to start a campaign to end poverty now. The moment we wake up and realize that slavery didn't go away but simply evolved, we think *somebody has to do something. If not me, then who?*

It's the question white people love to ask. I don't say it with a finger of judgment pointed at anyone else. This is my confession, even if it is not my sin alone: the blindness from which Jesus has been healing me for two decades is a peculiar one. Its primary temptation is to make me believe that I can see on my own—that I'm not, in fact, a blind man at all.

Racism thrives on the lie that I don't need the people my life depends on—that they, in turn, don't need me in a relationship governed by justice. The wages of whiteness, it turns out, is a loneliness in which individuals are damned to face the greatest challenges of life on our own. At the very center of this hell are those whose isolation is combined with power, deluding them into believing that the fate of the world depends on their hard work and good judgment.

Such was the hell I aspired to in Senator Thurmond's office. Racial blindness, racial habits, and racial politics conspired to propel me headlong into an abyss that I imagined as a mountaintop. I was entangled in a mess that I could not comprehend, much less unravel. But God was gracious enough to offer me a hand in the person of Rev. Barber.

The true and living God does not deal in abstractions but meets people personally, offering a way forward, not as a step-by-step itinerary but as a journey in the company of unlikely friends. That way is not the same for each of us, and it often seems to take a circuitous path, bringing us back to ground we thought we'd already covered, revealing things we missed the first time around. It is, like the Scriptures say, a ladder stretching from this fallen world to the heavens—a gift from God, inviting us to a place we've never yet been. But as enslaved people in America sang on the edges of plantations, Jacob's ladder is a spiral stair. "Every round goes higher, higher."

Reaching ahead with one hand and back with the other to grab the hand of someone else, those of us who chose to follow Jesus in this way join a circular dance through time. *We* are climbing—all of us, together—in an effort that requires courage and determination, for sure, but that is not, ultimately, about any one of us. This is the beloved community—the black-led freedom movement that has been here all along, even if many of us were too blind to see it.

Rev. Barber's hospitality became my personal link to a tradition that I learned was not unique to him. This was the river Uncle Vincent talked about, a rich source of wisdom that flowed through this land, ignored most of the time by people taught to imagine themselves as white or middle class. This is where both a radical vision and prophetic fire for reconstruction have been kept and passed down from one generation to the next. Here I've found a reconstructed gospel that offers real hope for America, for the church, and for my own sin-sick soul.

Saving the Soul of America

Before Dr. King was assassinated in Memphis, Tennessee, in 1968, he called Ebenezer Baptist Church, where he served as an associate minister, and provided a title for his sermon the next Sunday—a sermon he would never get to preach though he had been working toward it on the road for several weeks. King gave as his text the story of Lazarus and the rich man from Luke's Gospel. His title: "Why America May Go to Hell."

Just thirteen years earlier, at his first church out of seminary and graduate school, King had been swept into the river of prophetic resistance by Rosa Parks and her friends—Joanne Robinson, Fred Gray, and E. D. Nixon among them—who had been organizing for years to confront segregated busing in Montgomery, Alabama. Their bus boycott, which was successful after more than a year of nonviolent struggle, both sparked the modern civil rights movement and made Dr. King its spokesperson.

Montgomery taught King two things that led him to martyrdom in Memphis twelve years later. First, he learned that nonviolent love in action was the only force strong enough to overcome the demonic power of racism in America. Second—and the reality of this lesson became clearer with each step toward his cross in Memphis—King saw how the "principalities and powers" mentioned in Scripture have a death grip on our society. As he and many others prepared in the spring of 1968 for a Poor People's Campaign that would dramatize for the nation the divide between rich and poor, the story of Lazarus and Dives became a parable that spoke to the soul of America. Dives didn't go to hell, King began to say, because he was rich. He went to hell because he could not see his neighbor, Lazarus.

Dives went to hell because he was blinded by so-called privilege. And America, too, would go to hell, unless she made a concerted effort to correct the systemic economic injustice created by generations of stolen labor.

Half a century later, King's prophetic words speak directly to a tumultuous political climate in which growing income inequality pits so-called conservatives and liberals against one another in a zero-sum struggle where people on one side of any hot button issue cannot see people on the other side as fellow human beings. Donald Trump did not create this tumult, and he was certainly not the first politician to exploit it for political power. But his ascent to the White House did clarify how, in a deeply divided America, the victory that many white Christians celebrated as God's blessings was for sisters and brothers on the other side of our racial politics a descent into hell.

Most white folks didn't see this coming. Every Martin Luther King Jr. celebration through the Obama years felt like a chance to celebrate that, whatever our differences, we had stepped forward toward a postracial America. Rev. Barber, on the other hand, had been intentionally preparing a diverse coalition to resist Trumpism for a decade.

In 2006, after becoming the leader of the North Carolina NAACP, Rev. Barber began reaching across the lines of racial politics to build a new state-based political coalition. The NAACP, he noted, wasn't just an organization for black people. When it was first started in 1909, it was mostly *white* people who worked with W. E. B. DuBois and a handful of other African Americans to confront lynching and white supremacy in American politics. Rev. Barber was eager to teach people who cared about justice what his father had taught him: that the key to overcoming the divide-and-conquer tactics of white supremacy is *fusion politics*.

Here in North Carolina, the lesson of fusion politics was written in our Reconstruction history. When Redemption's white supremacy campaign overthrew federal Reconstruction throughout the South in 1877, control of state government returned to the plantation class, who restored Confederate-era governor Zebulon Vance to his former seat of power. In the 1880s, however, black Republicans in North Carolina found common cause with poor white farmers in the Populist movement. Their new "fusion" coalition built enough power to win control of the legislature, the governor's mansion, and both US Senate seats. Twenty years after the end of Reconstruction, North Carolina had produced a homegrown multiethnic democracy that wasn't imposed by federal authority but was supported electorally by a majority of its black and white citizens. This was the fusion politics that Rev. Barber wanted to reintroduce in the twenty-first century.

But he also knew that fusion politics had been violently attacked in 1898. Democrats employed a white-supremacy campaign that included voter intimidation tactics taken straight from the Mississippi Plan of 1876 to take North Carolina's government back from this fusion coalition. When they failed to win in Wilmington, the state's largest city at the time, an armed white militia ran elected officials out of office at gunpoint, murdered dozens of black citizens in the street, and burned down most of black-owned Wilmington. After their coup d'état was complete, white Democrats called for law and order.

Rev. Barber knew both the power of fusion politics and the determination of established powers to resist it at all costs. When he began inviting people into a twenty-first-century fusion coalition, he was both hopeful about the potential for a Third Reconstruction in America and honest about its costs. America's First Reconstruction was violently overthrown by a white supremacy campaign. Our Second Reconstruction was attacked by the Ku Klux Klan, infiltrated by the FBI's counterintelligence program (COINTELPRO), and disrupted by the assassinations of Medgar Evers, Malcolm X, Martin Luther King Jr., and Robert Kennedy. Every Southern politician knew by the early 2000s, however, that demographics were trending against them. Within a generation, white people in America were going to become one among many minorities. Fusion politics and a Third Reconstruction, Rev. Barber saw clearly, were our only hope for a democratic future in this nation.

North Carolina's fusion coalition worked. Within two years of coming together around a shared moral agenda, we were able to expand voting rights ahead of the 2008 election and mobilize the most diverse electorate in North Carolina's history. At the same time, the Democratic Party nominated a black man for president. Our fusion coalition handed him all fifteen of North Carolina's electors, and he won the White House.

But Rev. Barber was clear—this victory wasn't about one man. Barack Obama was not a messiah candidate who could redeem America. But his election did crack the Solid South, which had consistently delivered the South's electors to the Republican Party since Strom Thurmond led the Dixiecrats into the GOP in 1968.

Fusion politics helped me see what I had missed as a young white Christian. The power structure that had used Christianity to justify slavery, to fuel Redemption, to bless Jim Crow, and to bolster White Citizens' Councils had not gone away. After 1968, it had simply stopped using racialized language. Kevin Philips, chief architect of Nixon's Southern strategy, mastered the political art of demonizing poor and black people with code words such as entitlement programs, law and order, and state's rights. Good Christian white people could politely vote for candidates who perpetuated white supremacy while feeling good about donations to support urban ministries or our multiethnic reconciliation ministries, where we were careful to never be too political.

If anyone raised the race question, we knew they weren't talking about us. After all, we knew black people in our schools and in our workplaces. We weren't afraid of them. Surely we couldn't be racist.

Meanwhile, political operatives focused the incredible power of faith to motivate people for action on a very narrow set of moral issues, which could be manipulated to rally us at election time. Nothing worked better than abortion. The "Christian" vote wasn't about which candidate, regardless of party, offered policy proposals that moved us imperfectly toward the deepest values of Scripture. That would be too complicated. Instead, the "Christian" vote was framed as candidates who opposed abortion, claiming to be pro-life even as their policies were often detrimental to the lives of poor and black people in America. I, along with millions of other white Christians in America, was sold the stale bread of racism in this sweet and simple packaging of the Moral Majority.

Rev. Barber and fusion politics ushered me into a different kind of moral movement, where faith compelled people to ask deeper and more honest questions of themselves and of their elected representatives.

Moral Mondays

When the Solid South cracked in 2008, people whose wealth and power depend on our existing social structures got scared. These superrich families, who've been the beneficiaries of America's growing income inequality for decades, invested millions of dollars in North Carolina state politics. "They don't fight you when you're weak," Rev. Barber said. Resistance to fusion politics, he insisted, was a confirmation of its power.

By flooding state legislature races with cash, extremists bought candidates and took over the machinery of the state Republican Party, taking control of the North Carolina General Assembly in 2010. In their first legislative session, the new majority immediately redrew voting districts. In 2016, a federal court would rule that their power grab was an unconstitutional "racial gerrymander," which created apartheid districts by stacking and packing African Americans in a few districts they would win easily in order to dilute their ability to vote in fusion coalitions across districts. But long before the court ruled, their scheme worked. They won a supermajority in the legislature as well as the governor's race in 2012, while also electing a sympathetic majority of judges to the state supreme court.

Thus the 2013 legislative session in North Carolina became a policy template for the twenty-first-century Redemption movement. They started by cutting taxes, especially for the state's wealthiest citizens, then proceeded to cut government services in the name of fiscal responsibility. Such budgetary issues are, of course, what politicians argue about all the time. But the reactionary force of the North Carolina GOP's crusade to "take back our government" propelled them to attack things that Republicans had traditionally supported, like the Earned Income Tax Credit and public schools.

Then, after the most radical makeover of state government since the coup of 1898, our legislature passed the most extreme voter suppression bill since the 1960s, designed to make it more difficult for fusion coalitions to vote them out of power. Three years later, a federal court would rule that they had targeted African Americans with near "surgical precision." But as long as they had the power, they were determined to do everything they could to hold onto it.

All of this was done politely by people who talked about values and integrity. Good church people prayed for folks who were dying because they couldn't get insurance or public school teachers who were losing their aides. But they weren't sure what more they could do. Their faith might lead them to be genuinely concerned, but it didn't offer many resources for resisting extremism.

Then, during the Easter season of 2013, Rev. Barber and six other pastors, along with ten other North Carolinians, went into the rotunda of our statehouse and began to name what was happening there as immoral. They read from our state constitution, and they read from the prophet Isaiah:

> Doom to you who legislate evil,
>> who make laws that make victims—
> Laws that make misery for the poor,
>> that rob my destitute people of dignity,
> Exploiting defenseless widows,
>> taking advantage of homeless children. (Isaiah 10:1-2
>> *The Message*)

They were arrested that third Monday in April for raising a moral objection to extremism. The next Monday, hundreds of people showed up, and twice as many were arrested for not following building rules. By the next week, over a thousand people packed two floors of the legislature building. Moral Mondays became the largest state-government focused civil disobedience campaign in US history, with over twelve hundred people eventually arrested as tens of thousands of North Carolinians showed up weekly to bear moral witness at our statehouse.

In the halls of power, Moral Mondays made fusion politics into spiritual practice. This wasn't normal partisan politics. Something deeper was going on. Fusion politics had challenged racial politics, and white supremacy was fighting back with a vengeance. To pray quietly in our churches and minister to those who were hurting wasn't enough. The prophets of Scripture called us, like Jeremiah, to "go down to the palace of the king" (Jeremiah 22:1). A revival broke out, and our statehouse lawn was transformed into a camp meeting where the most diverse congregation I've ever witnessed gathered weekly to hear testimonies, sing freedom songs, receive a word of truth and justice, then answer the altar call by walking the aisle and going to jail. Hundreds said with their bodies, "I'd rather sacrifice my personal freedom than be silent while extremism takes over our government." And as the buses drove us to jail, thousands chanted, "Thank you, we love you!"

Moral Mondays became a national news story in the summer of 2013, but it didn't change anything for almost four years. "We need a movement, not a moment," Rev. Barber had said at the very first gathering of this fusion coalition in 2006. A decade later, when extremists lost control of two branches of North Carolina's state government, even as Donald Trump won the White House in the fall of 2016, political strategists began to take note of what Rev. Barber had been saying for a decade. A national polling agency based in North Carolina did a four-year analysis of public opinion and concluded that Moral Mondays had turned the tide three years earlier.

As American Christians grapple with the realities of racial politics—many of us for the first time in our adult lives—fusion politics offers us a form of moral witness in the way of Jesus. I believe, because I have seen it, that moral-fusion organizing can change the public conversation about our shared life in America. But, long before we saw the change we wanted, we had to keep going despite the lack of measurables in our favor.

Because fusion politics is rooted in the faith of the black-led freedom movement, it offers people recovering from the illusions of whiteness a public witness to heal the wounds of racial politics. You don't need to be a card-carrying Klan member or a cynical operative of the Southern strategy to be shaped by racial politics. Until the first time I walked into the General Assembly, willing to risk arrest as a moral witness, I didn't realize how much deference I carried in my body for the authority of that place. When an officer asked me to leave, my body wanted to listen. To be compliant felt like the "Christian" thing to do.

But fusion politics had connected me to people who suffered because of the compliance of Christians like me—to generations who had cried out when no one but God would hear them. Faithful witness, this tradition showed me, was about learning to feel that long struggle in my body—to sing its songs and hear its prophets and know that the freedom they promised was ultimately my freedom too. In public witness, a deeply personal formation was happening. Jesus was inviting me to walk the way of the cross with him.

The Way of the Cross

However we understand the saving work of Jesus' death and resurrection, the way of the cross that Jesus walked here on earth is a form of political engagement. Racial blindness has kept generations of white Christians in America from noting this basic feature of a story we've prized and memorized. But enslaved Christians couldn't miss the good news of a distinctive way toward freedom in Jesus' cross. Black social Christianity has always noted the political call of the gospel, even as that call has been interpreted and practiced in markedly different ways. AME Zion bishop Rev. Alexander Walters, who was instrumental in the founding of the NAACP, called Jesus, "the inspirer of all the reform movements of the world."

For those not blinded by racism, Jesus came to change more than individuals' hearts or the culture of families. Jesus came to change the world. He did it by gathering together a fusion coalition of the poor and the sick, tax collectors and zealots, religious defectors like Nicodemus, and lepers who had been written off as unclean. Preaching the good news that God's politics made room for all of them together in a new social order, Jesus built a popular movement in Galilee and throughout the Judean countryside that ultimately led to a nonviolent uprising in Palm Sunday's Triumphal Entry. The political threat of this popular movement got Jesus arrested and killed.

But for anyone who had been listening, this should not have been a surprise. In Luke's telling of the gospel story, Jesus has a heart-to-heart with his inner circle as soon as they begin to realize that he is the Messiah the prophets had foretold. "Whoever wants to be my disciple must deny themselves and take up their cross daily and follow me," Jesus says (Luke 9:23).

For generations of white evangelicals who were blinded to the political implications of this basic teaching, "taking up your cross" meant bearing with a particularly annoying person at the office or enduring the in-laws at Thanksgiving dinner. In the evangelical subculture, "suffering for Jesus" became a self-effacing way of admitting that, as a matter of fact, the life one was living was not really a challenge—a subtle way of confessing that missionaries who lived without easy access to peanut butter were the ones really "taking up their cross."

White Christians who have felt guilty about their "cross," agonized over whether they were doing enough, and practically worshiped the image of heroes who bear a cross they could never imagine. But for all the attention we've given this central teaching of Jesus, racial blindness has kept us from seeing what everyone in the first century knew as a fact of life: the cross is a consequence of confronting political power.

Enemies of Rome were crucified in first-century Palestine, just as enemies of the state are hunted down, locked away in prisons, blown up by drones, attacked by Navy Seal teams, and dumped in the open sea today. Charity may very well demand that you bear with your in-laws or refrain from speaking harshly to a coworker. But that is simply a consequence of negotiating normal human relationships. A cross is what you're forced to carry after you've been identified as an enemy of the established social order. Jesus says that when we join his movement, we'll face daily consequences of this social nonconformity.

After hundreds of people got arrested, went to court, and learned to live with a criminal record as a result of Moral Mondays, Rev. Barber read the Gospels to help us understand our daily lives. Jesus turning over the tables in the temple was the first Moral Monday, causing many who had supported him to walk away and drawing the ire of the authorities. But even as Jesus was on fire for justice, raging against economic injustice in the public square, he loved his enemies, forgiving them for their ignorance. The way of the cross showed us that we were going to have to face some dark Fridays before we tasted Sunday's resurrection.

This way of the cross offered a realism that never capitulated to compromise while it also offered hope in the here and now. Jesus offered a real alternative to the pious otherworldliness of the Pharisees, the cynical cooperation of the Herodians, and the political realism of the Sadducees. Likewise, Rev. Barber was well versed in the theological traditions of political social engagement in American Christianity. Reinhold Niebuhr's Christian realism suggested that love of neighbor sometimes required cooperation with an evil system to get things done and prevent greater evil. Evangelical pietism had imagined devout individuals each doing what was right in his or her own sphere of influence, sparking a chain reaction for the greater good. Postliberal theology, critical of the ways Niebuhr had led Christians to try to wield governmental power, pointed Christians toward small, countercultural experiments that bore witness to God's kingdom.

As the Spirit moved people to take up their cross through Moral Mondays, each of these traditions was stretched and challenged by the gospel speaking to our present. An evangelical pietist told me how, when he was teaching the book of Daniel to middle school boys at his church, it suddenly occurred to him that Daniel was arrested for civil disobedience when he defied an unjust law. Maybe Moral Mondays were creating some new Daniels.

Some mainline Protestants and secular agnostics who had shied away from bringing their religion into the public square admired how Rev. Barber's preaching kept people going, lifting their spirits even when they felt like they were fighting a losing battle. And many of us resident aliens from new monastic communities and postliberal congregations realized that, in our absence, extremism flourished in statehouses across the nation. Yes, the crusaders of the Christian Century lacked humility in the early 1900s. But so did we at the end of the century. We didn't need to walk away from politics; rather, we needed to submit to the leadership of people like Rev. Barber.

No, the kingdoms of this world were not going to become the kingdom of our God overnight. As a matter of fact, we learned that they were going to fight us tooth and nail. But in the struggle, fusion politics gave rise to a moral revival that connected us to people we had been separated from for generations. When we all got together, we saw a glimpse of the future that God has for us. What's more, we met the people our racial habits had kept us from knowing as friends.

9

HAVING CHURCH

★

The election of Donald Trump was a seismic event in the Christian social imagination, laying bare the wound of racial politics in America's congregations. Pastors who had assumed politics was either above their pay grade or simply off limits at church found themselves shepherding people who had been pitted against their neighbors by a campaign that never ended. On TV and in news feeds, Franklin Graham suggested that God, not the Southern strategy, had installed President Trump as a modern-day Nehemiah.

Rev. Barber, who diagnosed racial politics as America's "heart problem" in a speech to the 2016 Democratic National Convention, also framed Trump's rise in biblical terms. Rather than a Nehemiah restoring the ancient foundations, he read Trump as Nebuchadnezzar building a gold-plated tower and insisting that others bow down to worship him.

In the fall of 2016, 81 percent of white evangelicals didn't think they were bowing to an idol when they cast their ballots. In keeping with the messaging of generations, many values voters focused on abortion, naming as their top priority a conservative Supreme Court nominee. Others came out to "drain the swamp," to confront the corruption of political elites, or even to express their anxiety about an economy that promises less for their children than it did for them. "I don't like either of the options," a Mennonite in Ohio told me. "But I'd rather gamble on something different than vote for the same old thing."

For people across the racial divide, however, Trumpism *was* more of the same. Whatever African Americans thought of Obama's policies—the subject of many vigorous debates—people of color experienced the Obama years as a peculiar interruption to the status quo of white supremacy in America. Our president was black. It bears saying again: *our president was black.* The unimaginable almost began to feel normal. After JaiMichael's conversation with Pa at Easter dinner, during that final spring of the Obama era, it occurred to me: *my African American son has never known an America where a black man wasn't president.*

But JaiMichael's experience—along with that of a whole generation of young people—is an anomaly in American history. Both Republicans and Democrats regularly accuse the other side of being *divisive* in American public life. But this book has tried to both expose and examine the fact that *we have been divided for a long time.*

White-led churches have not, by and large, called Americans out of a society divided by race. More often than not, they have reinforced it. From slave evangelization to Redemption to calls for moderation when the Supreme Court ordered desegregation with "all deliberate speed," the Christianity of the slaveholder has, in a literal sense, prevented people who called themselves Christian from becoming church.

In the Greek of the New Testament, "church" is *ekklēsia*—"the called-out ones." To be called out of the patterns and practices of this world's sinful and broken systems into the economy of God's grace is to *become church*. To participate in an institution called *church* that nevertheless reinforces this world's broken systems is something far more cynical. I'm tempted to call it a country club for the middle class, but the country club is less tortured. Its members do not have to grapple weekly with a text and a tradition that have the power to liberate us from our self-imposed slavery, if only we would believe.

Any honest grappling with the Christianity of the slaveholder and the Christianity of Christ must, in the end, face the fact that white Christians in this land called America are the inheritors of tortured institutions, many of them rich in property and tradition, which nevertheless have experienced precious little church. What hope is there for such institutions? I hope by now the answer is plain enough—by God's grace, a church *did* emerge on the edges of plantations in the American South. In it, people who had not called themselves Christian retold stories they had learned to read in the holy book of their enslavers. Then and there, out in the unsanctioned brush arbors, they started having church. And people have been having church in America ever since.

None of these gatherings was perfect, and we have nowhere to go to find "the true church" today. The African American holiness church in your city is as likely to accommodate its members to middle-class mediocrity through prosperity preaching as the all-white megachurch down the street, with its musical selections carefully chosen to match the most popular local radio station. The Christianity of the slaveholder has shaped everyone's imagination in America. But in any place "where two or three are gathered together in [Jesus'] name" (Matthew 18:20 KJV), there is the potential that the Spirit can empower real people in our real world to interrupt the patterns we've inherited. This is happening all around us, all of the time. Learning to distinguish between the Christianity of the slaveholder and the Christianity of Christ gives us eyes to see how we can begin having church wherever we are.

Building Up the God Movement

I hadn't followed Rev. Barber's leadership into fusion politics very far before I heard the objection from fellow Christians that has echoed through the American church since white Southerners accused America's first public black preachers of political religionism during Reconstruction. "Why doesn't he focus on evangelism and the work of the church?" sincere Christians would ask. "If the Moral Majority was too political, isn't Rev. Barber being just as political on different issues?"

To anyone who suggested Moral Mondays were simply a shill for Democrats, I'd point out that Rev. Barber started organizing a fusion coalition in North Carolina when Democrats controlled our state government. But the more I heard their question, the more I realized that most people weren't wrestling so much with their vision of the body politic as they were with their understanding of the body of Christ. They weren't searching for a model of faithful public engagement. Instead, they were trying to defend the only model of church they'd ever known. So I started taking people to visit Greenleaf Christian Church, where Rev. Barber pastors.

In Goldsboro, North Carolina, across the tracks from downtown and the neighborhoods where most people think important things are happening in this eastern North Carolina town, Rev. Barber has taught and practiced for a quarter century the faith that was passed down to him. When he came to the congregation in the mid-1990s, they already had plans to grow the church by adding on to their existing church building. In their imagination, church growth meant more people, and more people meant a larger space. Faith was trusting that God could make a way for the bank to lend the money and for the people to pay the mortgage.

Rev. Barber asked the church leadership to come with him on a retreat. Together, they read Jesus' first sermon in Luke's Gospel:

> The Spirit of the Lord is on me,
>> because he has anointed me
>> to proclaim good news to the poor.
> He has sent me to proclaim freedom for the prisoners
>> and recovery of sight for the blind,
> to set the oppressed free,
>> to proclaim the year of the Lord's favor. (Luke 4:18-19)

If this was Jesus' first sermon, Rev. Barber asked, what does it tell us about the priorities of his earthly ministry? And how should it shape our vision for what we're doing as a church in Goldsboro?

For African Americans who had been faithful church members all their lives, it was a transformative conversation. In so many ways, they had assumed that what white folks called church was what they were supposed to be doing too—even if in a different style. The basic goal was the same: building up an institution that justified itself by the number of people who showed up to receive spiritual nourishment. Whatever material ministry the church engaged in was secondary to this mission. No one could deny that Jesus calls us to feed the hungry, clothe the naked, heal the sick, and visit the imprisoned. But those works of mercy had been imagined as auxiliary ministries, dependent on the central mission of building up a spiritual institution. No one had ever made this case to them. It's simply what they understood when they heard the word *church*.

But what if church was something else? What if it was the movement Jesus invited people into when he invited them to join together in "setting the oppressed free"? What if evangelism was inviting others to join this movement and church work was organizing local efforts to keep the movement moving?

Jesus' first sermon guided the leadership of Greenleaf toward a new definition of mission. They got out a map of Goldsboro, drew a circle with a two-mile radius around the building they already owned, and said, "This is where we're called to set the oppressed free. Whatever is enslaving people, we commit to fighting it by the power of the Spirit."

Over the next decade, a congregation of about 150 people invested $1.5 million of its own money in community development projects that brought over $10 million of investments into their neighborhood. They partnered with state and local government, businesses, congregations, and individuals to build fifty-six single-family homes, forty units of subsidized senior housing, a restaurant, and a community center, which houses a preschool, an after-school program, a gang-prevention program, and a reentry program for people coming home from prison. And twenty-five years after their leadership retreat, they still haven't built a new sanctuary.

A pastor who went with me to visit Greenleaf—to hear this story from some of the people who've lived it—confessed on the ride home, "That is the most faithful local ministry I've ever seen. Yet I've sat quietly and listened as fellow Christians who saw Rev. Barber for fifteen seconds on TV accused him of not doing the work of the church."

Rev. Barber and Greenleaf's witness have helped that pastor, me, and thousands of others see clearly how gospel practices fundamentally interrupt the racial habits that are too often perpetuated in church communities. When church growth isn't about how many people show up for services, but rather how many oppressed have been set free, then building a new worship space isn't as important as building a movement.

Jesus only had twelve disciples, but in the unlikely mix of the small group he gathered around him, we can see the patterns of a movement that interrupts America's racial habits. Matthew, the tax collector—a federal employee—broke bread with former Zealots, who would be on any terrorist watch list today. Fundamental to fusion politics, which extends far beyond any church or creed, is this gospel practice that leads us into surprising friendships. By endeavoring to live as Christ lived in the world, the church helps everyday people see and remember that another way is possible.

Gospel Practices for Having Church

Greenleaf's story helps us see and name the gospel practices that make church possible. Theirs is a story that grows out of the greatest miracle in American church history—the fact that people who weren't Christian, after being enslaved by people who called themselves Christian, somehow heard good news and discovered the Christianity of Christ in brush arbors and on front porches. Yet, like all gospel stories, Greenleaf's is a conversion narrative. Black skin—even the black church tradition in America—doesn't automatically grant anyone direct access to the Christianity of Christ. No congregation is untouched by the Christianity of the slaveholder; we're all called to conversion through *gospel practices.*

Still, we learn the moves and rhythms of gospel practices from those who've known Jesus for themselves. Such witnesses are plentiful in the river that flows from the forgotten places where enslaved people met the God who raised Israel out of Egypt. The faith-rooted, black-led freedom movement in America is the source of church renewal that generations of white-led institutions have longed for without having the eyes to see it.

For most of American church history, people who've told us the story of our faith believed that the church of the enslaved was inaccessible to us due to a lack of sources. Scholars know that, in the absence of evidence, humans tend to fill in the blanks of what we don't know, often with our own wishful thinking. Nostalgia is a powerful force. Historians keep us honest by insisting that we cannot dream about a true church in the past without sources to help us reconstruct its practices.

But in his groundbreaking book *Slave Religion*, Albert J. Raboteau made an incredible contribution to American church history. Once we clearly see the essential difference between the Christianity of the slaveholder and the Christianity of Christ, Raboteau's insight opens a door to faithful Christian practice more significant than any of the Great Awakenings that have swept across this nation's landscape. Raboteau put down in writing what he'd learned at his grandmother's knee—namely, that *the gospel of the enslaved church is preserved in its songs.*

While sound teaching can enlighten the mind and powerful preaching can move the heart, song has a unique power to move our bodies, pulling us into the river that flowed before us and will continue long after we are gone. The gospel practices that free us from our racial habits are not a set of exercises that will transform in thirty minutes a day. They are, rather, a way of life wrapped up in song. The central creed of this tradition—the faith that keeps me singing as I go—is called "I Will Trust in the Lord."

> I will trust in the Lord,
> I will trust in the Lord,
> I will trust in the Lord till I die.
> (Repeat)
> I'm gonna stay on the battlefield,
> I'm gonna stay on the battlefield,
> I'm gonna stay on the battlefield till I die.
> (Repeat)
> I'm gonna treat everybody right,
> I'm gonna treat everybody right,
> I'm gonna treat everybody right till I die.
> (Repeat)

It is not a complex song. Passed down through an oral tradition, it is easy to memorize. What's more, it doesn't need accompaniment. Like all the spirituals, "I Will Trust in the Lord" is both a melody you can hum while you walk alone and a song that leads us to harmonize when we are together. Its rhythmic emphasis isn't on the first and third beats, like the hymns and praise songs that come and go in white churches. Instead, it teaches us to clap on the second and fourth beats. This pattern, typical of the black gospel tradition, is more than a style that adds a soulful swing to our step. Its offbeat rhythm opens space in our life for improvisation. Our life flows on in endless song, yet no verse is exactly the same. This is a song to guide people who want to walk by the power of the Spirit in an unpredictable world.

"I will trust in the Lord . . . till I die," the song begins, introducing the *gospel practice of confession*. This creed begins with a confession that we are, each of us, willing to bet our lives on the way that led Jesus through the cross to resurrection. The bedrock reality that Greenleaf's leadership wrestled with on their retreat is precisely what every congregation of believers in Jesus Christ must grapple with: If Jesus is our Savior, will we trust him to be our Lord?

Far too many conversations about the renewal of the church in America focus on secondary issues of translating the gospel's message to new generations in a changing culture. I've sat with Episcopal bishops and evangelical grandmothers whose theologies (at least in the way we usually frame things) couldn't be further from each other. But they have this in common in twenty-first-century America: they worry that the church that has been a sanctuary from the storms of life for them will not be there for their grandchildren.

But before any message can be translated, it must be understood. The greatest threat to the gospel in America is not that it will be lost in translation; it's that it will be confused for the Christianity of the slaveholder. As such, it can either be dismissed as unhelpful baggage or be embraced as a set of beliefs that prop up the world as it is. But either way, it doesn't offer the gift of church—a people called out of this world's system into the life that is really life.

"I will trust in the Lord" is a confession that each of us must make for ourselves, but one that joins us together in a way of life that makes clear how faith means entrusting our lives to the God of the universe. We cannot save ourselves, and no idea or system of this world is going to save us either. Our foremothers in bondage could not hold their babies and whisper that everything was going to be all right unless they entrusted their well-being to a mystery beyond the plantation and its masters—beyond the world system that they knew. "I will trust in the Lord" was their confession, and it must be ours if we are to have church wherever we are today.

As we keep singing, the second line reminds us, over and over, that we cannot trust the God who brought Israel out of Egypt without engaging in a quarrel with the world. "I'm gonna stay on the battlefield," we sing, because our practice of confession necessarily flows into the *gospel practice of resistance*. This world's systems are not benign. They are captive to principalities and powers that oppress and kill. To trust Jesus is to join an army under siege. We are always already in the midst of a battle. The practice of resistance helps us learn how to stay on the battlefield.

For women and men who have been beaten down by this world's systems, this liberating good news straightens backs and steels the spirit. "Ain't gonna let nobody turn me 'round," they sing, glowing in the confidence of God. But for those of us who've inherited the so-called privilege of social power, the practice of resistance is an invitation to stay on the battlefield with sisters and brothers who have no choice but to be there.

The practice of resistance as "staying with" is an invitation to unlearn whiteness. Late in his life, the prophetic writer James Baldwin frequently asked white Americans to consider what their ancestors had given up in order to become white. When they were German or Irish or Greek, what did they leave behind in order to step into America's imagination of whiteness? To consider the question is to face the reality that whiteness isn't *real*. Yes, it shapes everything in America. But it is an illusion that not only denigrated and abused black people's bodies but also contorted white souls. When people who've imagined themselves to be white choose to stay on the battlefield with people of color, we learn that our freedom, too, is bound up in the victory that only God can bring. The practice of resistance, then, instills in us not a false sense of persecution but rather a solidarity with all who, against great odds, know that God is on our side.

The final verse of this creed speaks to all who have been drawn together into the river of resistance that Jesus called a "kingdom . . . not of this world" (John 18:36). In the midst of the fight that we can neither avoid nor back down from, we sing, "I'm gonna treat everybody right." The *gospel practice of nonviolent love* instills in each of us a resolve to not fight the way this world's systems teach us to fight.

By simple observation we learn that, in most any conflict, the side with more money, more people, and better technology wins in this world. It's why Greenleaf thought they needed to build that new and better sanctuary. It's why I though I needed to become president of the United States for Jesus. The basic logic of this world's systems will whisper to us at every turn, "If you really want to make a difference, you have to overwhelm the enemy."

But Jesus saw, just as Gandhi and Martin Luther King Jr. did after him, that we cannot dismantle the plantation system with the ways and means of the master. Any oppressed person can feel that oppression is wrong. History suggests that no group of people can wield power over another without, at some point, having the guns turned back on them. (Witness, as a single example, the fact that plantation owners paid pastors to teach enslaved people to read the Bible until Nat Turner organized his revolt in 1831. Shortly thereafter, it became illegal throughout the South to teach an enslaved person to read.)

But flipping a system on its head does not fundamentally change the relations of the people within it. This is why the revolutionary love ethic of Jesus presents a radical alternative in the history of the world. When we sing, "I'm gonna treat everybody right," we echo generations of people who've prayed for their enemies, even as they stood on the battlefield, refusing to bow down.

The gospel practice of nonviolent love comes to life in communities of people who know that, whatever the challenge they face, they cannot allow their adversary to become the enemy. Yes, gang violence may frighten a community. But the young men with the guns aren't gangsters. They're some grandmama's baby, some mother's son. We need them, just as we need the police officer who has been taught to fear a whole community, patrolling someone else's neighborhood as if it were enemy territory. To say Black Lives Matter is not to say that officers' lives don't matter. It is to commit ourselves to stand with people who are being killed until we can, together, win police officers as our friends.

This does not happen all at once. Often, it feels like it will never happen at all. But every verse we sing ends with "till I die." We trust in the Lord, stay on the battlefield, and treat everybody right *until we die* because, frankly, nonviolent love can get you killed. We know the stories of martyrs like Dr. King. But God only knows the stories of the millions buried in the woods and at the bottom of the sea. This is not a song to make you famous, but a faith to sustain you when you go to jail, when the money runs out, when you are powerless and cold and alone.

You sing this song, and you know you're not alone. You've been invited into something big enough to hold all your sorrows. You've become a living member of the body of Christ.

All Things Are Possible with God

The gospel practices of *confession*, *resistance*, and *nonviolent love* are not, as I said, an exercise plan that will transform your church in thirty minutes a day. But that doesn't make them any less practical than a strategic planning process or 40 Days of Purpose. These practices are simple steps that any group of people can take to move toward having church. But *simple* doesn't mean *easy*. By any honest account, they are hard.

In Mark's Gospel, after the series of stories about how the blind learn to see, a man of so-called privilege—let's call him a middle-class American—comes to Jesus, asking for practical instruction. "What must I do to inherit eternal life?" (Mark 10:17).

Jesus' reply is not complex. He reviews the basic creed of Israel, the way of life with God that is summed up in the Ten Commandments. But this middle-class American is stuck in his blindness. He wants more. These practices seem too simple. Child's play, he calls them. "All these I have kept since I was a boy" (Mark 10:20).

I know the feeling. Surely, if the good way were so simple, our history would not be as tortured, nor our present so fraught with division. Between the Christianity of the slaveholder and the Christianity of Christ there is the widest possible difference, I know. And yet I have loved and been loved by people who still cannot see the *Brown v. Board of Education* decision as anything other than unrighteous meddling in "our Southern way of life." *It was never about race. It was always about our right to decide how and where we want our children to be educated.*

We are well practiced in self-deception. If we recall that no single issue for a quarter century after *Brown v. Board* was more important to white Southern Christians than segregation, it's much less confusing why our various denominations have been in turmoil for the past decade over how the church should respond to homosexuality. We are well practiced in self-deception.

Still, Jesus insists that the remedy is simple. Practice the way of life God has outlined for you, and you will live. When the middle-class American whines that this plan is too simple (it will never work!), Jesus doesn't scold. "He looked at him and loved him," Mark says. Jesus makes an honest assessment of the situation, then names the next step in gospel practice for this brother. "Go, sell everything you have and give to the poor" (Mark 10:21).

Don't build the new sanctuary. Quit your job. Trust yourself. Forgive the one who hurt you. Go and meet the gang member. The next step for any of us is as particular as our context and the stories that have brought us into the relationships where we are. But the rich young ruler wouldn't have been talking to Jesus— just as you wouldn't be reading this book—if he didn't already sense something of what the next step in gospel practice would mean for him.

Mark says the rich young ruler "went away sad" when Jesus invited him to take the next step (Mark 10:22). We don't know if he remained sad the rest of his life or if, somewhere on the way home, he unloaded his riches on some lucky soul and started to live the life God made him for then and there. For Mark, the main thing wasn't how this man responded, but how we will respond when the choice is before us. The next step is often straightforward. But it's also hard.

Jesus repeats himself to make the point: "How hard it is to enter the kingdom of God!" (Mark 10:24).

Which compels the disciples to ask on behalf of all of us, "Who then can be saved?" (Mark 10:26).

It's not a comfortable place to be—this free fall without a bottom during which we feel in the gut that's caught in our throats how incapable anyone of us is to find our way out of the mess that we have inherited. All Christians confess a doctrine of original sin, but nothing I've experienced makes me feel its reality down deep in my bones like the challenge of discerning slaveholder religion from the Christianity of Christ. A simple distinction, yes. But hold your life alongside these two Christianities and the choice you're left with on any given day is as hard as cold steel. "Who then can be saved?"

"All things are possible with God," Jesus says (Mark 10:27). It's a simple statement of faith. But Jesus fleshes out its content for his disciples by saying "no one who has left home or brothers or sisters or mother or father or children or fields for me and the gospel will fail to receive a hundred times as much in this present age" (Mark 10:29-30).

Yes, gospel practices will cost us everything. But when we give ourselves to gospel practices, we gain what we could not have otherwise: "homes, brothers, sisters, mothers, children and fields—along with persecutions—and in the age to come eternal life" (Mark 10:30). We can begin to live the life that's really life—not some ideal (persecutions come right along with it!), but a beloved community that starts now and lasts forever. In short, when we trust the gospel's practices, letting them direct our lives, we begin to have what the New Testament calls "church."

10

HEALING
THE HEART

★

Twenty years ago, Jesus interrupted my racial blindness and exposed, as my experience in the plantation chapel would later help me to name, that I'm a man torn in two.

I get it honest. I was both born into an economy built on race-based slavery and baptized in a church that broke fellowship with sisters and brothers who said God was opposed to slavery. White supremacy isn't something I chose, but I have to own it. It is my inheritance. In this, I am not alone. The world system that was literally fleshed out on this land that I call home is what we all now call the global economy.

By God's grace, I was invited into a church that offers a real alternative to the patterns and practices of this death-dealing system. My life in that beloved community has ushered me into a moral movement that not only offers the possibility of a better politic but also connects me to beloved community beyond my own faith tradition—a confluence of streams that make up that great river Revelation images as the chief corridor in the *polis* that is to come, right here on earth as it is in heaven. But I would be less than honest if I tried to chronicle the political and ecclesial hope that reconstructing the gospel offers without facing the personal struggle at the heart of this book.

I am a man torn in two. The only gospel that can be good news to me is one that has the power to touch me down on the inside and heal the hidden wound that rends my soul. Reconstructing the gospel can never only be about the individual. This is why so many noble efforts at reconciliation fail. They pretend that broken people with the best of motives can simply opt out of hundreds of years of history through individual choices and relationships. Such relationships are necessarily dishonest, both because they ignore the real material conditions that weigh on people's lives and because they offer a false sense of relief from white guilt, which keeps people like me from facing the hidden wound of our whiteness.

Whenever we try to start with the personal work of reconstructing the gospel, the individualism of the faith we've inherited almost guarantees that we miss the essential context of our personal conversion in community. But if we stop short of the personal work—if we deceive ourselves into thinking that we can reconstruct the gospel without addressing our divided souls, then we carry the germ of white supremacy with us into our most noble efforts to rid this world's systems of racism. Nothing is uglier than the inevitable explosion when white people try to participate in antiracist work without addressing their own hidden wound. Each of us has to do our own soul work.

In his first church out of seminary, where Rev. Barber experienced the struggles of pastoring a church while trying to build a fusion coalition with others in the community, he had a wise deacon who would whisper in his ear occasionally and help him keep his bearings. During a public-education campaign about environmental racism, Rev. Barber expressed his frustration with some of the white allies in the community. They talked the talk about solidarity in the struggle, but when it came time to make public demands, they capitulated to those in power, not feeling the same sense of urgency as did black folks who knew their lives and community were on the line.

"Here's what you've got to understand about white folks," the deacon said to Rev. Barber. "At the end of the day, their choice isn't whether the cause is just. What they've got to decide is whether their mama lied to them."

When Rev. Barber told me that story, I knew he was talking to me. My inheritance of white supremacy isn't an asset that I can simply take up or put down—it is not a privilege that I can leverage for any cause. It is, like any inheritance, tied up with relationships of trust (or mistrust) that shape not only how I imagine the world but also how I conceive of who I am.

No one wants to call his or her mama a liar. I am who I am because my mama loved me. If anyone even suggests that she has less than the purest intentions, my gut tells me to fight them. But if, in the painful reality of our shared history, I must confess that she (and others) passed down lies to me that were passed down to her, that not only shifts how I see the world, but it also affects our relationship; it touches the most intimate place inside of me.

This is the unspeakable source of the tears that well up when we white people choose not to run or fight but to face our inheritance—to accept the basic difference between the Christianity of the slaveholder and the Christianity of Christ. I've heard white people confess it through sobs dozens of times: "I'm sorry . . . I just don't know how to say it . . . I don't know what's come over me." Some have called this "white fragility," and they are right; faced with the same hard facts that people of color have never been able to avoid, white people don't have the resources for resilience that have kept black people alive in America.

But for white people who have learned to think of themselves as naturally in control, the rare experience of vulnerability introduces the possibility of the essential soul work that might lead to conversion. It is not the job of people who've borne the burden of white supremacy to hold our hands and wipe our tears as white people endeavor to do this work. And yet, it is a deep irony of the story in which we find ourselves, that the well-being of the planet very much depends on white people doing this work.

No one saw this more clearly than James Baldwin, who prophesied the extremism of the twenty-first century by simply observing the patterns of white supremacy that had, despite moral resistance, persisted throughout his lifetime. "The crisis of leadership in the white community is remarkable—and terrifying—because there is, in fact, no white community," Baldwin observed. "America became white—the people who, as they claim, 'settled' this country became white—because of the necessity of denying the black presence, and justifying the black subjugation. No community can be based on such a principle." The inevitable end of whiteness is self-destruction, Baldwin saw. But such a demise is of concern, even to people with next to nothing to lose, because we're all in the same ship now. If plantation capitalism simply goes to hell, we go down with it in the global economy, which is why each of us has to do our soul work.

The personal work of letting a reconstructed gospel heal my hidden wounds isn't just about saving me. It's about doing what I can, in the network of relationships that I was born into, to accept God's saving grace for the whole world. While none of us can do this work alone, it may well be that no work to reconstruct the body politic or the body Christ can be complete until white people deal with the division each of us embodies.

The Shriveled Heart Syndrome

When Moral Mondays brought people together on our statehouse lawn in the summer of 2013, I saw a lot of people week after week who I'd not met before. One of them was an old white man who seemed particularly jubilant—especially for someone of his generation—to be part of a black-led freedom movement. I remember watching one evening as moral witnesses who'd been arrested were ushered onto a prison transport bus in handcuffs. A young black man, who was holding a bullhorn outside, led the crowd in a chant: "You're gonna need another bus / 'cause baby, there are more of us!" He held a fist of resistance in the air. And right there beside him, this old white man did the same.

Eventually, Rev. Barber introduced me to the white man, Bob Zellner. Bob had relocated to North Carolina the year before after learning about Rev. Barber's leadership. He was one of the seventeen people arrested on the first Moral Monday. Why had he been so eager to join?

Bob told me about going to college in Montgomery, Alabama, in 1957. When his sociology professor at an all-white Methodist school, Huntington College, asked Bob to write a paper on "the race problem," Bob decided to learn about the local bus boycott, which had successfully desegregated Montgomery's buses in 1956. Journalists had come from all over the world to tell the story. Bob figured he could go across town and interview Dr. Martin Luther King Jr.

But his professor said, "No, you'll be arrested." Bob went anyway, and after a daylong nonviolence workshop at the First Baptist Church, Dr. King informed Bob and a few fellow white students who'd come with him that the church was surrounded by police. They said they planned to arrest the students who had violated the Jim Crow laws by attending a meeting with black people. "Wow, that's what our professor said would happen," Bob commented. "That's why he's a professor," Dr. King replied with a smile.

At the church that day, Bob recalls Rosa Parks saying to him, "You can't study a problem forever. When you see something that's wrong, at some point you have to do something about it." Bob joined the Student Nonviolent Coordinating Committee (SNCC) in 1961 and was the last white member to leave when it became an all-black organization. But Bob never left the movement. He was in North Carolina in 2013 because he knew that the antiracist work Dr. King and Ms. Parks had welcomed him into continued. If it was happening in North Carolina, that's where Bob was going to be.

I asked Bob what it had been like for him, a white man from the Deep South, to join the civil rights movement. "Well," Bob said, "Granddaddy was in the Klan, and Daddy had been in the Klan, but I think the thing that made it possible for me to become a human being was that Daddy left the Klan when I was a boy. Mama cut up his Klan robes and made dress shirts for us boys. We may be the only little Southern white boys ever to have gone to Sunday school in shirts made from Klan robes."

Bob said his granddaddy and his uncles never spoke to his daddy again after he left the Klan. To hold on to their view of the world and of themselves, they had to disown their flesh and blood. He didn't comprehend the pain of that rejection until later in life, but Bob said it helped him to understand the white men who nearly beat him to death in Mississippi, as well as the officers who arrested and jailed him dozens of times in the 1960s.

Eventually, Bob came to the conclusion that, as a group, white people suffer from a malady that he calls the "shriveled-heart syndrome." It is rooted in the experience of white people enslaving black people. "Slavery is an act of war," Bob said. "You can't maintain it without violence." If black people were to be kept in slavery, they had to become an enemy. That meant cutting off any empathy that arose from witnessing the suffering of a fellow human being.

But you can't shut up compassion in a human heart one minute and then go back to normal the next. Trauma science has taught us that even short-term experiences of war or violence can lead to long-term posttraumatic stress, affecting someone's ability to function in intimate relationships. Generations of committing an act of war against a group of people would have to have equally long consequences. But we've hardly known how to name them. Just as laws and customs are passed down, one generation to the next, shriveled-heart syndrome has become part of white people's shared inheritance. It's a way of naming how we've been torn in two—why those tears flow with inexpressible emotions when we try to face real issues of race.

But diagnosing any malady is important because, to some degree, the way toward healing always emerges from our understanding of the problem. If racism were simply the problem of white people being separated from black people, then the way toward healing would be simply to spend more time together. If it were only a structural problem, arising from some unforeseen error, then policy changes alone could have some hope of correcting it. But if the white supremacy that has compromised our churches and created the conditions for annihilation of the planet is rooted in the shriveled hearts of millions of people who imagine themselves to be white, then personal practices to heal the heart are needed. This is the soul work that each white person must commit to do, each and every day.

Practices of the Heart

In the long history of the church, across many different cultures and long before the lie of race was introduced in the modern world, Christians recognized that all human institutions become entangled in this world's systems. Jesus challenged the temple cult of his day, just as prophets after him would arise to call people out of religious hypocrisy into true and living faith.

The church calls these prophets saints, and many of our traditions recognize that their essential role is *monastic*—that is, singularly focused (*mono* means "one") on living the way of Jesus. Of course, monasticism is practiced by human beings and thus subject to the corruption of white supremacy in all the ways that any human institution is. But the calling of the monastic is to lead a life of repentance—a "perpetual Lent," Saint Benedict, the father of Western monasticism called it.

True repentance is never about beating ourselves up. White guilt can easily become the self-flagellation of a monasticism that has lost its way, but true repentance turns our hearts toward the love of God, compelling us to chase after the gospel life, no matter the cost. The monastic knows that a man in a cave can be closer to true wisdom than a tenured professor at the world's best university. Monastic wisdom, then, is particularly helpful for people in America who want to unlearn whiteness, with all of its middle-class assumptions, in order to embrace the Christianity of Christ.

For the past fifteen years here in Walltown, where Sammie helped me see my racial blindness and Ms. Carolyn invited me into the fellowship of her front porch, Leah and I have lived a "new monasticism" with other recovering white people. We relocated to a historically black neighborhood and a historically black church to live a life of repentance because, more than anything, we wanted God's love to heal our shriveled hearts. This is where I do my soul work day in and day out.

Saint Benedict, who fled Rome when it was the center of world power to pray in cave on a mountainside, discovered once he arrived that there was already an old man named Romulus, who knew the gospel's truth. Evidently Benedict hadn't made a plan for how to survive. Romulus fed him. Our experience 1500 years later has been similar. While we came here focused on what we needed to flee from, with little plan for how we would survive, we were welcomed by black sisters and brothers who already knew the gospel way. They showed us that Psalm 118:22 is true: "The stone the builders rejected has become the cornerstone." God has already given us everything we need to heal our shriveled hearts.

You can feel it sitting on Ms. Carolyn's porch, laughing on the corner with Sammie, or singing "I Will Trust in the Lord" with the male chorus at Saint John's Missionary Baptist Church, where Deacon McCrea, in his mid-nineties, still remembers how his grandmother who survived slavery measured out each line. But just as Benedict spent three years in the cave, then lived the rest of his life in the way of penance that he learned there, we've learned that our hearts grow through daily, personal practices.

At the end of his life, Benedict looked back and realized that the gospel way that Romulus had passed down to him consisted of three basic practices, which echo throughout the Scriptures: *listening*, *staying put*, and *constantly reforming your life*. These central practices of the monastic life, which are summed up in the Benedictine vows, help me name what I've learned as a new monastic about turning from whiteness toward the freedom of life in Christ.

"Just shut up and listen" might be the most important instruction for anyone committed to unlearning whiteness. A shriveled heart, I know from experience, cannot listen well. In conversation, it interrupts to make a point. In daily life, it often prefers distraction to genuine engagement with God or other people.

But those who know they are blind learn to trust their ears. I've learned to see a great deal over the past twenty years, and that seeing is important. But much more important—and this is what I have to ground myself in each day—is a commitment to listen. When I read the Bible each morning, I don't just ask myself, "What do I hear the Spirit saying?" I ask, "What does Rev. Barber hear? What does Grandma Ann hear?"

A decade ago, when Barack Obama had to reject his pastor in order to run for president, I'd just published a book on what white evangelicals can learn from the black church tradition. In every interview I gave after that book was published, someone asked, "So, do you think white Christians need to leave their churches and join black churches?"

"No," I said every time. "I'd never wish that on the black church!" But the question itself revealed how unimaginable the notion of submitting to black leadership is for most white Christians in America.

I don't think all white people need to leave their churches to join others led by black people—and not only because it isn't going to happen. But because even if it did happen, black folks know that the white people would take over eventually. And whether they do or not, the patterns and practices of whiteness have shaped every church in America. The line between the Christianity of the slaveholder and the Christianity of Christ doesn't run between black churches and white churches. It runs through them—and through each and every one of our souls.

The personal transformation that is essential for each of us is *listening*—and listening, in particular, to the voices of those who have been rejected because of their blackness. Whether it's the prayer warrior at your local AME church or the Black Lives Matter activist you meet at a local protest, white people need to cultivate the daily practice of listening to that person. We listen not only to hear where they are coming from but also to understand who we are in a world we share, though our experiences of it are vastly different.

Without a practice of listening to enlarge our hearts, it really doesn't matter how much our lives are desegregated. Every Southern white man for generations, when confronted with the charge of racism, has replied, "Some of my best friends are black."

The fact of the matter is that life on most plantations was less segregated than much of the daily experience of white people in America today. But proximity did not lead to understanding. Indeed, the hearts of white people shriveled through generations of forced intimacy in which the cries of whipped black men and raped black women were ignored.

It's not enough to be in relationship. White and black people have a long history of relationship. For healing to begin, we must learn to listen with our hearts.

This is where the monastic practice of *staying put* becomes so important—because we white people don't know what to do with our vulnerability. White fragility, while real, is more the exception than the rule. We're more accustomed to white rigidity—to clearly defined roles and responses. We know precious little about lament.

This is where funerals in Walltown have been a formative experience for me. I grew up in a tight-knit white community in rural North Carolina. We knew most people for several miles around. If a member of our church died, we attended the funeral, always on the third day after death. If the person was part of another congregation, we usually visited the family at the funeral home on the evening of the second day. If you couldn't make it to either, you made a commitment to stop by the home.

In white communities like ours, death was a relatively predictable part of life that we'd learned to deal with. Not so in Walltown. Through Jim Crow and the War on Drugs, this community has been stalked by death. I'll never forget the evening I argued with a young man I'd known since he was a boy, trying to convince him that "if you live by the gun, you'll die by the gun." He told me he knew that by the time he was twenty-one he was going to be in the grave or in prison. It wasn't a matter of if, but of when. If a gun could help him survive one more day, he was going to use it.

To be saved in such a context isn't to be free from the ever-present threat of death. Though it reminds us that another world is possible, the church is not an escape from the troubles of this world. In Walltown, black people die—too soon and too often. While the movement has invited us into a struggle that challenges this systemic injustice, the saints of our local congregations have taught me how to lament as I stay put.

In Walltown, we put off the funeral until everyone can get here—sometimes a week or more. People travel from up and down the East Coast, retracing the paths of the twentieth century's Great Migration, when African Americans fled the terror of the South, mostly for the ghettos of urban centers along the Eastern Seaboard and in the Midwest. The casket is open at the front of the church as people arrive, and I've watched mothers throw themselves on sons taken from them, just as daughters have clung to mama's hand crying out in agony. Lament takes time. I've never seen a pastor in Walltown try to hurry anyone through this process. Any funeral can last hours, and after the body has been buried, family and friends often linger at the church house—and later in homes—into the night. No one pretends to know how grief works. But folks hold onto one another and cry. They do not rush back to work, for which many of them are paid by the hour.

This staying put—*stabilitas*, the monastics call it—is the practice shriveled hearts need to heal from their white rigidity. No, it is not the responsibility of black people to hold our hands as we look into the abyss that is our inheritance and will be our legacy if we are not completely born again. Black churches cannot play grief counselor for Christians who carry the hidden wounds of the Christianity of the slaveholder. But, if we are willing to listen, they can be our teachers.

A commitment to stay put helps us learn the humility that is impossible when we are praised for solving the problems we think we understand. If history teaches us anything, it is that our predicament goes much deeper than any solution we can imagine. This reality scares white people, who have been taught to imagine, above all else, that we are in control of our world. When we give ourselves to work led by people of color, we have the opportunity each day to practice the patience and stability that can expand our hearts.

But this staying put isn't the opposite of action. It is the necessary counterbalance to faithful action in solidarity with people who are suffering. "We used to tell white people they needed to check their privilege when they come to work with us," a black pastor told me years ago. "So they stopped coming. Now they go on mission trips to Africa instead." Rather than do the hard work of staying put, whiteness tempts us to believe that our efforts will be of more use (or more appreciated!) somewhere else.

The practice of *constantly reforming our lives* becomes essential for the healing of our hearts in the places and relationships we inhabit. No, we can't just do something. And yet, each of us must do something to respond faithfully to the people we've heard and the lament we have engaged. Each step we take is both insufficient and inadequate, especially when held against the overwhelming power of whiteness. But that doesn't make the next step in our healing any less necessary. Quite the opposite. As Benedict said, with the Scriptures as our guide, we must "run on."

"You have to risk something," Bob Zellner told me. Because when you risk something in solidarity with those who've suffered the brutality of white supremacy, you don't only learn what it means to struggle. You also learn how that struggle reorients your relationship to the people and institutions who've always treated you as another white person. The first time Bob marched with SNCC in McComb, Mississippi, he was the only white man in a march led by local students from the African American high school. Local white folks immediately focused their attention on him as an outside agitator. They became even more enraged when they heard in his voice that he was a fellow Southerner. His action didn't just change his relationship with the black folks who were teaching him another history of the South. It fundamentally changed the way other white people saw him. For over a decade, an intelligence officer of the state of Alabama followed Bob anytime he crossed the border into his own home state.

But you don't have to narrowly escape being lynched to risk something. Show up where you're a minority. Take some of the wealth that you inherited with your whiteness and help the local AME Zion church pay off its mortgage. Tell your friends why you can no longer vote with the good white Christians for every Republican candidate on the ticket.

Nothing you can do is going to change the world. But that's no reason not to do it. If you spend a night in jail, standing up for what is right, you may not change anyone's opinion on the issue. But *you* will change—and not only in your own estimation. Your public action will compel every person who knows and loves you to reconsider how whiteness has taught them to imagine the world.

As black folks know all too well, there's no guarantee that they will listen. There's no guarantee that anyone—not even your closest loved ones—will stay put and face the fundamental difference between the Christianity of this land and the Christianity of Christ. But when you've come to the place that you are ready to take a risk, you know all too well the feeling in their gut that keeps them trapped in their whiteness. And, what is more, you know something of the freedom that comes when you let go of your whiteness and let God, as the prophet Ezekiel said, "remove from you your heart of stone and give you a heart of flesh" (Ezekiel 36:26).

A LETTER TO MY GRANDFATHER AND MY SON

★

*D*ear Pa and JaiMichael,
    Sitting across from the two of you at dinner last Easter, I witnessed an impasse that is not uncommon in America. We hear almost every day that we live in a divided country, yet the dinner tables where we rub elbows across this acknowledged chasm are few and far between.

We've always celebrated a determination to stick together despite disagreement, both in our family and in this nation. It's why we love Dr. King's "I Have a Dream" and Jesus' "love one another as I have loved you." However real our differences, we hold onto hope that we have more in common than that which divides us.

But the tug I felt in my gut as I watched the two of you struggling to understand each other was more than a worry that the experiment we know as America may not endure. Something between nausea and hunger, that feeling has returned in the dark of each morning as I've tried to build a bridge of words between your worlds—something to span the breach that racism created, a gulf that I feel at the center of myself.

Pa, you taught me to sing the songs of faith. I often hear your tenor when the organ is playing in a church, before the congregation begins to sing.

I realized how deep those songs were in my spirit when you were a little boy, JaiMichael. After I'd read to you each night, we'd say our prayers and turn out the light. Back then you always wanted me to stay, so you'd ask for a song. "Softly and tenderly, Jesus is calling," I started singing. You wanted it every night. I passed on to you what was passed down to me.

We are weary people in a wounded world, and Jesus is calling us home. I know it is true, and I've seen enough to trust that God can make a way out of no way to get us there. But we are not home yet, nor have we ever been. Most of the social sins that have been committed in our tortured history have been perpetrated by Christians. "All have sinned and fall short of the glory of God" (Romans 3:23) we say, and it is true. But we practice self-deception if we do not acknowledge that the worst of these sins were done in the name of God. From Easter Sunday at the Colfax Courthouse to our family's Easter dinner, we are a people divided by faith.

While it is clarifying to distinguish between the religion of the slaveholder and the Christianity of Christ, the fact remains that there is nowhere we can go to learn and practice the pure and unadulterated Christianity of Christ. White supremacy has shaped us all, though in markedly different ways.

JaiMichael, you have no choice but to learn what it means to negotiate this world as a man who others see as black. Those who came before you stood tall to say that black is beautiful and that black people deserve the same political and economic power that all other people deserve in our world. You are the person God made you to be, and you must not let any person or institution lead you to think otherwise. But they will try over and again because the same evil forces that tell you it is wrong to be black have spent centuries telling me and Pa and millions who resemble us that it is good to be white. Not only good, but godly.

Whiteness, I have learned, is a religion. It is fueled by its power to give those who believe it a sense of worth. And for anyone who needs it, it is a faith that must be sustained in spite of the evidence. No one can be persuaded that the belief that tells them who they are isn't true. I know this from experience. But I have also known the friendship of brothers and sisters who loved me out of the lie that is written across each of us. Most of them have been black, their experience of white supremacy giving them a personal connection to the God who raised Jesus from the dead after raising Israel out of Egypt. But some have also been of a lighter hue, for the Scriptures are true: our God is no respecter of persons.

Even white people, I have seen, can be saved. But not on our own. Of this, I am certain. Earnestly, tenderly Jesus *is* calling us home. He has demonstrated his commitment by making a way out of no way, through the cross. But we cannot follow Jesus to glory without accepting the new humanity of his body here and now. I've written this book for the same reason I'm writing to you—because I do not want to miss this gift, and I want to share it with both of you and all of our sisters and brothers who long for a better story that tells us who we are.

I love you both,
Jonathan (Dad)

ACKNOWLEDGMENTS

★

The black-led freedom movement has long insisted that there are two things white folks need to learn: when to shut up and when to speak up. One pitfall of whiteness is thinking you always have something important to say. Anyone who publishes a book about anything is subject to this temptation. But on the other side of the narrow way that leads to life is an equally perilous precipice—the danger of silence when you are the one who must speak up.

If I've come anywhere close to balancing what sometimes feels like a tightrope stretched across hell, it's because of the love of people I name here . . . and many others I don't. The author gets to choose which stories to tell, but he also knows the ones left untold, some of which shape him more than he can say. I offer my deepest gratitude to those who know grace and have shown it to me. You know who you are.

As a writer, I'm also indebted to fellow writers and thinkers who've helped me tend to the words and ideas. For their help and encouragement on this project, I especially thank Charles Halton, Kathryn House, D. L. Mayfield, Tim Tyson, Daniel Camacho, Will Willimon, Bishop Hope Morgan Ward, Tomi Oredein, Abby Norman, Shane Claiborne, Christi Dye, and Al Hsu. My thinking is also dependent on ongoing conversations (and conversion) with my colleagues at School for Conversion. Thanks to Louis Threatt, Sarah Jobe, Dan Keegan, Jennifer Jones, Scott Adams, Will Elmore, Bob Zellner, Luke Everett, Gann Herman, Byron McMillian, Taylor Lewis Guthrie Hartman, Keith Daniel, Miea Walker, Ross Houser, Debbie Buffaloe, and Steve Swayne.

I'm inspired these days by my work with Repairers of the Breach and pray that, in some small way, this book serves our larger mission of building a new Poor People's Campaign to revive the heart of democracy and save the soul of America for the sake of our sisters and brothers throughout the world. Thanks to all the staff and my fellow board members at Repairers. If you don't know them, you should: breachrepairers.org.

This book is dedicated to the Reverend Dr. William J. Barber II, president and senior lecturer at Repairers of the Breach. He is not only Beatrice to this divine comedy, loving us toward beloved community, but also a prophet to America in our time. I thank God for him, and for the community that makes leadership like his possible.

I want to thank Bill Cahoy and the Lilly Endowment for sponsoring the Vincent Harding Community Builders cohort, a dozen pastors and Christian professionals who reflected with me for two years on the kind of leadership that makes it possible for ordinary people to resist slaveholder religion and build up beloved community. Our work together helped me see both why this book was needed and how I could write it.

I'm also grateful to the Fund for Theological Exploration (FTE) and the North Carolina Conference of the United Methodist Church for partnering with School for Conversion to develop our 21st Century Freedom Ride program into a vocational discernment process for young clergy. Teaching Southern history to young clergy has helped me clarify the scope of what reconstructing the gospel entails. This book certainly doesn't cover it all, but I do want to thank the hundreds of people who've engaged in this conversation with me while traveling the back roads and hallowed ground from eastern North Carolina to lower Alabama. I pray our conversations will continue and include others we've not yet met as we strive to become the people we've not yet been.

This is not a history book, a Bible study, or a racial equity workbook, but the teacher in me knows that the church needs more—and better—of all these. Still, as a writer I know that too much of any of these can kill the little something inside of you that keeps you turning the page. If you're still reading here at the end of the book, I've done my job as an author.

At least, I hope I have. A writer keeps you reading by crafting a lasso out of words, then looping it around your heart. He tugs you from one chapter to the next, maybe even persuading you to go places you would not have wanted to go. The writer cannot know you well enough to tell you what to do next, but if he has done his job, you want to do something. If he has done it well, you know you must.

The endnotes that follow, annotated by the teacher in me, offer guidance toward further reading, organizations, and trainings that may help you find your way. For those interested in beginning the journey from slaveholder religion toward the

Christianity of Christ, these endnotes are intended as a curriculum for Conversion 101. Share them with your Bible study, Sunday school, family, and friends. Use them to start a freedom circle in your living room—or to find your way to a freedom movement in your city. God is reconstructing the gospel and wants each of us to do our part. I'd love to hear what you decide to do.

NOTES

I Christmas on the Plantation

13 *our family, black and white*: Paul Cameron's papers are archived in the Cameron Family Papers #133, Southern Historical Collection, Wilson Library, University of North Carolina at Chapel Hill. An illuminating history of the Cameron family's unsuccessful attempt to recover an enslaved "family member" who escaped to freedom is available in Sydney Nathans, *To Free a Family: The Journey of Mary Walker* (Cambridge, MA: Harvard University Press, 2012).

One Lord, one faith: The Rev. Brooks Graebner was quoting, as preachers are wont to do, from memory (Ephesians 4:5-6).

15 *The power of the master must be absolute*: The State v. John Mann, 13 N.C. 263 (1829). Legal scholar Mark V. Tushnet has chronicled this case and its impact on the American legal system in *Slave Law in the American South: "State v. Mann" in History and Literature* (Lawrence: University Press of Kansas, 2003).

17 *institutional racism*: The insight that racism is a structural reality is inherent in the black-led freedom struggle since Reconstruction. See W. E. B. DuBois, *Black Reconstruction in America: 1860–1880*, introduction by David Levering Lewis (1962; repr., New York: Free Press, 1998); and Eric Foner, *Reconstruction: America's Unfinished Revolution, 1863–1877*, updated ed. (New York: Harper Perennial, 2014). The term *institutional racism* was coined by Stokeley Carmichael (Kwame Ture) to name the fundamental structural issues he faced firsthand in the civil rights movement, which many historians now frame as a Second Reconstruction in America's history. See Kwame Ture and Charles V. Hamilton, *Black Power: The Politics of Liberation*, with new afterwords by the authors (New York: Random House, 1967; New York: Vintage Books, 1992), 4.

17 *white applicant with a criminal record*: This is one of the more striking findings of sociologist Devah Pager's extensive research on discrimination in hiring. "Being black in America today is just about the same as having a felony conviction in terms of one's chances of finding a job," she writes. See Devah Pager, *Marked: Race, Crime, and Finding Work in an Era of Mass Incarceration* (Chicago: University of Chicago Press, 2007), 91.

18 *African American veterans of World War II didn't benefit*: No one has chronicled systemic racial disparity in contemporary America more compellingly than National Book Award winner Ta-Nehisi Coates. The story of Clyde Ross makes this particular point. See Coates, "The Case for Reparations," *Atlantic*, June 2014. The perpetuation of systemic inequities that Coates and others have chronicled is central to any understanding of institutional racism. Racial-equity training—as opposed to cultural-sensitivity training—is designed to help individuals and institutions learn to see and discuss systemic bias. Any church or institution committed to reconstructing the gospel should actively pursue racial-equity training. Some great resources are the Racial Equity Institute (racialequityinstitute.org) and the Community Institute for Racial Equity, a program sponsored by the Race and Social Justice Initiative of Seattle, Washington (www.seattle.gov/rsji/community/campaign-for-racial-equity/community-institute-for-racial-equity).

19 *principalities and powers*: See Ephesians 6:12 (KJV).

Mary in the garden: See John 20:1-18.

2 Immoral Majority

26 *Colfax massacre*: The Easter Sunday coup d'état of 1873 in Colfax, Louisiana, was the single bloodiest day of the post–Civil War white backlash and is well documented in the literature on Reconstruction. Its role in the deeply religious Redemption movement, which overthrew Reconstruction in 1877, is chronicled in Nicholas Lemann's *Redemption: The Last Battle of the Civil War* (New York: Farrar, Straus and Giroux, 2006), 3-29.

27 *Dunning School*: The deconstruction required before any reconstruction can begin demands that we reconsider how we remember history. You don't have to know anything about the Dunning School to be shaped by it. During her presidential campaign in 2015, Hillary Clinton parroted the Dunning School thesis about Reconstruction, reflecting the history she would have learned in high school and college. Lamenting the death of her favorite president, Abraham

Lincoln, Clinton said, "I don't know what our country might have been like had he not been murdered, but I bet that it might have been a little less rancorous, a little more forgiving and tolerant, that might possibly have brought people back together more quickly. But instead, you know, we had Reconstruction. . . . We had people in the South feeling totally discouraged and defiant. So, I really do believe he could have very well put us on a different path." (See Zach Carter, "Why Hillary Clinton's Take on Abraham Lincoln Is 'Total Fantasy,'" Politics, *Huffpost*, January 30, 2016, www.huffingtonpost.com/entry/hillary -clinton-abraham-lincoln_us_56abcccbe4b077d4fe8e169b.) Contemporary scholarship, which has paid much more attention to the lived experience of formerly enslaved African Americans in the South, debunks the claim that Reconstruction failed because Radical Republicans were too extreme. Despite heroic efforts like the stand for democracy at Colfax Courthouse, Reconstruction was overthrown because the United States was not willing to confront a white-supremacy campaign. See Adam Fairclough, "Was the Grant of Black Suffrage a Political Error? Reconsidering the Views of John W. Burgess, William A. Dunning, and Eric Foner on Congressional Reconstruction," *Journal of the Historical Society* 12 (June 2012): 155-88.

28 *he knew we could not endorse him*: During his 1980 campaign for president, Ronald Reagan addressed the National Association of Evangelicals on August 22 in Dallas, Texas. "I know this is a non-partisan gathering, and so I know that you can't endorse me," he said, "but I only brought that up because I want you to know that I endorse you and what you're doing" (National Affairs Campaign address on religious liberty, available at American Rhetoric, www.americanrhetoric .com/speeches/ronaldreaganreligiousliberty.htm). Less than three weeks earlier, Reagan had rallied a crowd at the Neshoba County Fairgrounds, seven miles from where three civil rights workers were brutally murdered sixteen years earlier, with the words, "I still believe the answer to any problem lies with the people. I believe in states' rights." Rooted in the Redemption campaign of the 1870s, this combination of religion and slightly veiled white supremacy has been a hallmark of racial politics. Though Donald Trump has become infamous for crudely exploiting this strategy, he inherited it from generations of politicians before him. For a history of this Southern strategy in modern America, see Dan T. Carter, *From George Wallace to Newt Gingrich: Race in the Conservative Counterrevolution, 1963–1994* (Baton Rouge: Louisiana State University Press, 1996).

28 *Dr. King argued for a bigger war on poverty*: The battle over how Dr. King is remembered is, in many ways, the most contemporary and ongoing conversation about how we remember America's racial history. King's close friend Dr. Vincent Harding resisted the domestication of King from the very beginning of the Martin Luther King Jr. holiday. See his book *Martin Luther King: The Inconvenient Hero* (Maryknoll, NY: Orbis, 2008). Dr. Cornel West has also edited a volume of Dr. King's writings and speeches to highlight, as the title makes clear, the radical nature of King's vision. See Martin Luther King Jr., *Radical King*, ed. Cornel West (Boston: Beacon Press, 2016).

29 *Strom Thurmond*: Thurmond's political survival into the late twentieth century is a case study in institutional racism. He did not need to dislike black people in order to perpetuate white supremacy. In fact, it was widely known that the senator had an African American daughter in South Carolina. But intimate relationships with African Americans did not change his view of policies that perpetuated racial inequalities, one generation to the next. On Thurmond's role in the twentieth century, see Carter's *From George Wallace to Newt Gingrich*. For an analysis of how institutional racism is perpetuated without racial animus, see Eduardo Bonilla-Silva, *Racism Without Racists: Color-blind Racism and the Persistence of Inequality in America*, 5th ed. (Lanham, MD: Rowman & Littlefield, 2018).

30 *communities were gentrified*: *Gentrification* is a technical term for the displacement of poor people by the landed gentry. Because the Americas were gentrified by Europeans during colonization, property law in the United States has largely justified this displacement. Many journalists and scholars have noted that race (not simply class) played a central role in the determination of which low-income communities were gentrified after the civil rights movement. While many urban-core communities experienced white flight during this period, the reurbanization of America's cities has been the principle demographic shift of twenty-first-century America, bringing mostly white people who grew up in suburbs in close proximity to the mostly black and brown people who inhabited these inner-city communities. Indeed, while *urban* is still used as a euphemism for *black*, current trends in gentrification suggest that the connection will be lost on the next generation of Americans. I've found the insights of the psychiatrist Mindy Thompson Fullilove especially helpful in understanding the complexities of the historically black and currently gentrifying Walltown

neighborhood in Durham, North Carolina. See especially her books *Root Shock: How Tearing Up City Neighborhoods Hurts America, and What We Can Do About It*, 2nd ed. (New York: One World/Ballatine, 2005); and *Urban Alchemy: Restoring Joy in America's Sorted-Out Cities* (New York: New Village Press, 2013).

31   *#BlackLivesMatter*: I have worked closely with the local leadership of this movement in North Carolina and know and respect several of its leaders in other parts of the country. The Movement for Black Lives, as active participants refer to it, does not have a hierarchical structure with a single spokesperson. They proudly call themselves a "leaderful" movement. Sincere white evangelicals have called me to ask about rumors that #BlackLivesMatter is a terrorist organization. Anyone who knows the history of black-led freedom movements in this country can tell you that such accusations and blanket dismissals of a concerted effort for racial justice are commonplace. For anyone genuinely interested in learning more about the movement, its leadership, and the trajectory of their organizing, see Jelani Cobb, "The Matter of Black Lives," *New Yorker*, March 14, 2016. Keeanga-Yamahtta Taylor offers a deeply theological analysis in her book *From #BlackLives Matter to Black Liberation* (Chicago: Haymarket Books, 2016).

32   *campaign rally in Fayetteville*: John McGraw, the man who was charged with and convicted of assault for attacking Rakeem Jones at the Trump rally in Fayetteville, gave an interview to *Inside Edition*, in which he said, "He deserved it. The next time we see him, we might have to kill him" ("Trump Supporter Who Punched Protester: 'Next Time, We Might Have to Kill Him,'" *Inside Edition*, March 10, 2016, www .insideedition.com/headlines/15177-trump-supporter-who-punched -protester-next-time-we-might-have-to-kill-him). Though McGraw later apologized to Jones in court, he maintained (perhaps under legal advisement) that the attack was not racially motivated. Like rally-goers who insisted that their Confederate flags were about "heritage, not hate," McGraw did not call Jones a racial slur. He said Jones was "un-American" for insisting that black lives matter. See "Fingers Point in Many Directions After Attack at Trump Rally," *WRAL*, Linden, NC, March 11, 2016, www.wral.com/trump-s-rough-handling-of-rally -dissenters-stirs-questions/15514502/.

34   *I find, since reading over the foregoing Narrative*: Frederick Douglass, appendix to *Narrative of the Life of Frederick Douglass, an American Slave*, introduction by Eric Ashley Hairston (London: Quarto, 2017),

97-103. There are many editions of Douglass's narrative available, including online. One of the first widely read accounts of an enslaved person in America, the text has played a central role in the history of African American literature. A complex character who lived well beyond the end of slavery, Douglass's life offers a window on the black-led freedom struggle before, during, and after America's Civil War. For an engaging contemporary introduction to Douglass, see James Oakes, *The Radical and the Republican: Frederick Douglass, Abraham Lincoln, and the Triumph of Antislavery Politics* (New York: Norton, 2008). For those interested in making pilgrimage, the Frederick Douglass House, outside Washington, DC, is preserved by the National Park Service.

35 *Edward Snowden*: Snowden is a former Central Intelligence Agency employee who leaked classified information from the National Security Agency in 2013 without authorization.

Nearly a million people were massacred: Though overshadowed by news about O. J. Simpson when it was happening, the Rwandan genocide is well documented in several books and documentaries. Emmanuel M. Katongole grapples with the theological and ecclesial implications for Western Christians in his book *Mirror to the Church: Resurrecting Faith After Genocide in Rwanda* (Grand Rapids: Zondervan, 2009).

Pew Center data: "U.S. Religious Landscape Survey: Religious Affiliation," Religion & Public Life, Pew Research Center, February 1, 2008, www.pewforum.org/2008/02/01/u-s-religious-landscape-survey-religious-affiliation.

36 *Cleopas walks home after Passover*: See Luke 24:13-35.

3 Racial Blindness

46 Decision *magazine*: A publication of the Billy Graham Evangelistic Association, *Decision* magazine claims in its tagline to be "The Evangelical Voice for Today." While it is not uncommon for slaveholder religion to assert that white Christians speak for the whole church, the election of Donald Trump exposed in twenty-first-century America how *evangelical* is often simply a euphemism for white conservative. In order to follow Jesus in America, disciples must learn to see how slaveholder religion uses "Christian" institutions and messengers to subvert the Christianity of Christ. Kevin Kruse has chronicled many of the details of how this happened in the twentieth century in his book *One Nation Under God: How Corporate America*

Invented Christian America (New York: Basic Books, 2016). For quotations from Franklin Graham, see "From Franklin Graham: The Most Important Election of Our Lifetime," *Decision*, September 2016, 4-5. Other articles on religious liberty in the same 2016 Election Special issue were by David Jeremiah, Eric Metaxas, Joy Allmond, and Charles Chandler.

48   *George Freeman*: Bishop George Washington Freeman was a mainstream, respected white Christian in his own day, much as Franklin Graham is in America today. To hold their public witness alongside one another, two centuries removed on the very same soil, is to consider how slaveholder religion is real and present in contemporary American Christianity. For quotations from Bishop Freeman, see "The Rights and Duties of Slave-holders: Two Discourses, Delivered on Sunday, November 27, 1836, in Christ Church, Raleigh, North-Carolina," Protestant Episcopal Society for the Advancement of Christianity in South-Carolina, Charleston, 1837, https://archive.org/details /rightsdutiesofsl00free.

49   *Graham held a rally*: For quotations from Franklin Graham, see Tim Funk, "Franklin Graham Praises McCrory, Blames Charlotte for HB2-related Disruption," *News & Observer*, October 13, 2016, www.news observer.com/news/politics-government/election/article108054832.html. Raw video of Graham's speech, from which some quotations are taken, is also available here.

      federal court ruling: The quotation from a federal court ruling comes from NAACP v. McCrory (US 4th District Court of Appeals, NC, 2016). This decision was upheld by the Supreme Court in 2017.

50   *American Antislavery Society*: For the sake of a journey toward understanding, this book aims to unveil slaveholder Christianity before illuminating the Christianity of Christ. But both have always existed alongside one another in America, and you can rarely see the one clearly without reference to the other. For a popular introduction to the abolition movement of the nineteenth century, which was led by people of deep faith, see the docudrama "American Experience: The Abolitionists," a four-part series from PBS that is available, along with educational resources, at www.pbs.org/wgbh/americanexperience /films/abolitionists.

51   *Franklin Graham agreed to meet*: My account here is based on personal interviews with clergy from the NAACP who attended the luncheon

with Graham. An open letter to Graham was published on October 29, 2012. See Bob Allen, "NAACP Criticizes Franklin Graham," *Baptist News Global*, November 1, 2012, https://baptistnews.com/article /naacp-criticizes-franklin-graham/#.WTbpqDPMzow.

52 *Ku Klux Klan held a victory parade*: An increase in activity among white supremacist hate groups has been well documented by the Southern Poverty Law Center, which tracks more than 1,600 hate groups active in the United States today. Learn more at splcenter.org /issues/hate-and-extremism. For a report on the Klan rally in Roxboro, North Carolina, see Tammy Grubb, "Klan Parade Drives Through Roxboro, Opponents Rally Across State," *News & Observer*, December 3, 2016, www.newsobserver.com/news/local/counties/wake-county /article118735548.html.

At the center of Mark's Gospel: See Mark 8:22–10:52.

54 *Project Implicit*: Learn more about Project Implicit and test your own implicit bias at https://implicit.harvard.edu/implicit/takeatest.html. Like all vice, implicit bias is something people cannot simply opt out of because we think it's bad. It is an inherited habit and a pattern in our minds. But moral anthropology insists that humans can change, and the best neuroscience suggests a plasticity in the brain that lasts throughout human life. The single most important factor in changing implicit bias is regular and normal interaction with people who we have been taught, as a group, to fear.

55 *Levi Coffin*: For an introduction to Coffin and other figures in the Underground Railroad, see Fergus M. Bordewich, *Bound for Canaan: The Epic Story of the Underground Railroad, America's First Civil Rights Movement* (New York: HarperCollins/Amistad, 2005).

4 Living in Skin

57 *Tupac*: For background on Tupac Shakur and an introduction to his cultural analysis, see Michael Eric Dyson, *Holler If You Hear Me: Searching for Tupac Shakur* (New York: Basic Civitas Books, 2006).

58 *friends in low places*: Earl Lee and Dewayne Blackwell, "Friends in Low Places," Sony/ATV Music, recorded by Garth Brooks in 1990.

59 *Fingertips on the hips*: Gregory E. Jacobs, Roger Troutman, Shirley J. Murdock, Larry Troutman, Tupac Amaru Shakur, and Ronald R. Brooks, "I Get Around," Sony/ATV Music, recorded by Tupac in 1993.

59 *"Keep Ya Head Up"*: Darryl Anderson, Tupac Amaru Shakur, Roger Troutman, and Stan Vincent, "Keep Ya Head Up," Sony/ATV Music, recorded by Tupac in 1993.

60 *Closing of the American Mind*: Allan Bloom, *The Closing of the American Mind: How Higher Education Has Failed Democracy and Impoverished the Souls of Today's Students* (New York: Simon & Schuster, 1987).

61 *The sins of our fathers (and mothers)*: Intersectionality names how one kind of systemic oppression is necessarily tied (often in complex ways) to others. We cannot speak honestly about the abuse of black bodies without also understanding the use and abuse of female bodies and the control of other bodies considered alien, criminal, or queer. So I am, in a pointed way, asking us to face the sins of our *fathers*—the abuse of power that is consistently borne by people who don't conform to white male expectations. But this is not only a challenge to white men like myself who have benefited from power. To confess sin is to acknowledge that it is not a benefit but a deprivation. The intersectional sins that grow from white male dominance hurt us all. It is no accident that many of the most insightful voices in the Movement for Black Lives today are women. For a deeply theological perspective, see Kelly Brown Douglas, *Stand Your Ground: Black Bodies and the Justice of God* (Maryknoll, NY: Orbis, 2015).

   Joseph meant nothing: Read Exodus 1:8-22 to see how this new king enslaved the Israelites in Egypt.

62 *And before I'd be a slave*: Words taken from the African American spiritual "Oh Freedom."

63 *Now at one's feet there are chasms*: See Lillian Smith, *The Journey* (London: Cresset Press, 1955), 75. The chapter of Smith's memoir from which this quotation is taken begins, "What was Grandma afraid of? She did not know." Few writers in American history have grappled with the hidden wounds of whiteness as honestly as Lillian Smith. See also her books *Killers of the Dream* (1949; repr., New York: Norton, 1994) and *The White Christian and His Conscience* (1945; repr., Whitefish, MT: Literary Licensing, 2011).

65 *Thorton Stringfellow*: Though certainly not unique among white Christians in the mid-nineteenth century, Stringfellow was prolific in his defense of slavery. Between 1850 and 1861, he published three books toward this end. A century and a half later, he is remembered for little else. Quotes are taken from Thornton Stringfellow, *A Brief*

Examination of Scripture Testimony on the Institution of Slavery, in an Essay, First Published in the Religious Herald, and Republished by Request: With Remarks on a Letter of Elder Galusha, of New York, to Dr. R. Fuller, of South Carolina (Washington: Printed at the Congressional Globe Office, 1850). Accessed online at http://docsouth.unc.edu /church/stringfellow/stringfellow.html.

66 *Harriet Tubman*: Because she is scheduled to replace Andrew Jackson on the twenty-dollar bill, Tubman may become better known to twenty-first-century Americans than is Frederick Douglass, her fellow abolitionist, who received much more press and attention in the nineteenth century. WGN America's *Underground* devoted an entire episode to a Harriet Tubman "Ted Talk" in their 2017 season. Via subscription services online, you can view "Minty" (season 2, episode 6), a powerful introduction to this woman and her faith. The Harriet Tubman National Historic Park in Auburn, New York, a pilgrimage site for many who recognize this "Moses" of the faith-rooted freedom struggle, is a reminder that America's original sin is not simply a Southern story. If we have eyes to see, there are places hallowed by the black-led freedom struggle in every state and community.

millions of Ham's descendants: Stringfellow, *Brief Examination*, 55.

71 *submit herself graciously*: Southern Baptist Convention, "The Baptist Faith and Message," article 18, amended 1998, www.sbc.net/bfm2000 /bfm2000.asp.

Sarah Grimké: While the real heroes of America's black-led freedom struggle are almost always people of color, it is important to note that people who were taught to see themselves as white have also learned to see themselves and those around them in a different light. Sarah Grimké's conversion also inspired her younger sister, Angelina, who left the South to work alongside her sister in the abolitionist struggle. See Gerda Lerner, *The Grimké Sisters from South Carolina: Pioneers for Women's Rights and Abolition*, rev. ed. (Chapel Hill: University of North Carolina Press, 2004). A text of Grimké's "An Epistle to the Clergy of the Southern States" (1836) is available in various formats via a link on this website: http://antislavery.eserver.org/religious /grimkeepistle/an-epistle-to-the-clergy-of-the-southern-states.

5 This Is My Body, Broken

75 *WPA interviews*: The Works Progress Administration, in 1939 renamed the Work Projects Administration, was the largest American

New Deal agency. These interviews by staff of the WPA with women and men who had been enslaved are among the most important primary documents we have about the experience of chattel slavery in America. While scholars have noted that white and black interviewers often got different stories, much of the best scholarship on the cultural world of enslaved people is based on these interviews, published narratives, and stories and songs that were passed down orally. See Eugene D. Genovese, *Roll, Jordan, Roll: The World the Slaves Made* (New York: Vintage Books, 1976). The classic text about the faith that emerged in the brush arbors of Southern plantations is Albert J. Raboteau, *Slave Religion: The "Invisible Institution" in the Antebellum South*, updated ed. (New York: Oxford University Press, 2004).

76 *Baby Suggs*: While primary sources on the experience of enslavement are limited, the memory of what it has meant to be black in America is, as the front-porch experience suggests, a shared one. Toni Morrison is the literary genius who has best channeled that collective memory and imagination for others. Her novels span the African American experience, from slavery to the present. Though some white Christians have tried to have these books banned from public schools for addressing sensitive personal issues, they should be required reading for all inheritors of slaveholder religion. See Toni Morrison, *Beloved* (New York: Knopf, 1987), 88, for quotation.

77 *Racial habits*: For a more in-depth explanation and analysis of how racism is embedded in everyday habits, see Eddie S. Glaude Jr., *Democracy in Black: How Race Still Enslaves the American Soul* (New York: Crown, 2016), 51-70.

gap between the median incomes: This is a point emphasized by sociologists Christian Smith and Michael O. Emerson in their book *Divided by Faith: Evangelical Religion and the Problem of Race in America* (New York: Oxford University Press, 2001), 93-114. Anyone interested in a more systematic analysis of the intellectual categories evangelicals have employed to justify and perpetuate slaveholder religion (often unknowingly) should study Emerson and Smith's book.

78 *New Jim Crow*: Since writing her celebrated book, *The New Jim Crow: Mass Incarceration in the Age of Colorblindness* (New York: New Press, 2010), which focuses on racial disparities in our criminal justice system, Michelle Alexander has become a visiting professor at Union Theological Seminary. She is an important resource for Christians who want to be part of reconstructing the gospel.

79   *Richard Allen*: See Richard S. Newman, *Freedom's Prophet: Bishop Richard Allen, the AME Church, and the Black Founding Fathers* (New York: New York University Press, 2008).

      Denmark Vesey: See Douglas R. Egerton, *He Shall Go Out Free: The Lives of Denmark Vesey*, rev. ed. (Lanham, MD: Rowman & Littlefield, 2004).

      start a race war: Ray Sanchez and Ed Payne, "Charleston Church Shooting: Who is Dylann Roof?," *CNN*, December 16, 2016, www.cnn.com/2015/06/19/us/charleston-church-shooting-suspect/index.html.

82   *Dred Scott decision*: Dred Scott v. Sandford, 60 U.S. 393 (1857).

83   *Reconstruction meant something incredibly important for American Christianity*: In addition to the historical work on Reconstruction by W. E. B. DuBois, *Black Reconstruction in America: 1860–1880*, introduction by David Levering Lewis (1962; repr., New York: Free Press, 1998), and Eric Foner, *Reconstruction: America's Unfinished Revolution, 1863–1877*, updated ed. (New York: Harper Perennial, 2014), Gary Dorrien's work to chronicle the public Christianity of the black social gospel in postbellum America is deeply informative. He has published the first of a trilogy: *The New Abolition: W. E. B. DuBois and the Black Social Gospel* (New Haven, CT: Yale University Press, 2015).

      summed up their prophetic cry: Frederick Douglass, quoted in "The Anti-Slavery Society," *New York Times*, May 11, 1865, www.nytimes.com/1865/05/11/news/anti-slavery-society-exciting-debate-final-action-mr-gurrison-s-resolution.html?pagewanted=all.

      power concedes nothing without a demand: Fredrick Douglass, "West India Emancipation," Canandaigua, NY, August 3, 1857, www.blackpast.org/1857-frederick-douglass-if-there-no-struggle-there-no-progress.

84   *Thomas Dixon Jr.*: See Michele K. Gillespie and Randal L. Hall, eds., *Thomas Dixon Jr. and the Birth of Modern America* (Baton Rouge: Louisiana State University Press, 2006).

85   *Invisible Empire of defeated soldiers*: See review of *The Clansman*, by Thomas Dixon Jr., *Biblical Recorder: Organ of the Baptist State Convention of North Carolina* 70, no. 30 (February 1, 1905): 1, available from Special Collections & Archives, Z. Smith Reynolds Library, Wake Forest University.

86   *a well in Samaria*: See John 4:1-26.

88   *Freedom Summer*: See Bruce Watson, *Freedom Summer: The Savage Season of 1964 That Made Mississippi Burn and Made America a*

Democracy (New York: Penguin, 2011). Stanley Nelson's documentary, *Freedom Summer*, aired June 24, 2014, as part of the PBS American Experience series, is also a great resource for introducing others to this story. It is available online, with additional teaching resources, at www .pbs.org/wgbh/americanexperience/films/freedomsummer/.

6 A Gilded Cross in the Public Square

91   *The stone the builders rejected*: See Psalm 118, all of it. No Christian should ever sing "this *is* the day the LORD has made" (Psalm 118:24 NKJV) without knowing why we rejoice—because God has chosen rejected stones to finish off the work of reconstruction.

Ann Atwater: Ann's story is told by Osha Gray Davidson in his book *The Best of Enemies: Race and Redemption in the New South*, new ed. (Chapel Hill: University of North Carolina Press, 2007). A movie by the same name is scheduled for release in 2018.

95   *Honey, de white man is de ruler*: See Zora Neale Hurston, *Their Eyes Were Watching God* (New York: Harper & Row, 1990), 14.

97   *Black Power*: Stokely Carmichael and Charles V. Hamilton, *Black Power: The Politics of Liberation in America* (New York: Random House, 1967).

100   *Letter from Birmingham City Jail*: "Letter from Birmingham City Jail" is available as a primary document with accompanying teacher resources at www.teachingamericanhistory.org/library/mlk-jr.

Various problems which cause: "Letter to Martin Luther King" is available as a primary document with accompanying teacher resources at http://teachingamericanhistory.org/library/document/letter-to-martin-luther-king/.

Bull Connor: Theophilus Eugene "Bull" Connor was Birmingham's Commissioner of Public Safety for two decades and opposed the activities of the civil rights movement in his city in the early 1960s.

101   *Roman authorities arrest Jesus*: See Luke 23:1-25.

All four Gospels record: See Matthew 26:6-13, Mark 14:3-9, Luke 7:36-40, and John 12:3-7.

7 The Other Half of History

108   *My children, there is a God who hears*: See Sojourner Truth, *The Narrative of Sojourner Truth, A Bondswoman . . .* (Battle Creek, MI: Review & Herald Office, 1884), 17, http://docsouth.unc.edu/neh/truth84/truth84.html. An itinerant evangelist for the Christianity of Christ,

Truth was a mystic whose religious experience prefigures early Pentecostalism in America. PBS's *God in America* series offers good resources for introducing Sojourner Truth: *People & Ideas: Sojourner Truth*, www.pbs.org/godinamerica/people/sojourner-truth.html.

109 *Frederick Douglass*: Frederick Douglass, *Narrative of the Life of Frederick Douglass, an American Slave*, ed. Philip Smith (1845; New York: Dover, 1995), 34.

109 *William Lloyd Garrison*: White people who are committed to the journey from slaveholder religion to the Christianity of Christ must resist the very white temptation to think that we are pioneers facing uncharted frontiers. Many have stumbled along this way before us, finding real freedom and making mistakes that do not have to be repeated. For several years I taught a course at Duke Divinity School with Emmanuel Katongole and Chris Rice called Journeys of Reconciliation. We introduced our students to often little-known stories of directly impacted people who have led the struggle for justice in this history of the church. As I listened to our students, I heard a persistent question: Where does a middle-class white person like me find a role in these stories? The answer is, almost always, not out front. But those who inherited the so-called privilege of whiteness can (and must) play a role. Though he did not always get it right, Garrison spent his life both trying to find that role within the abolitionist movement and articulating to others like him what he could see. We would all do well to learn from his experience. For a good biography of Garrison, see Henry Mayer, *All on Fire: William Lloyd Garrison and the Abolition of Slavery* (repr., New York: St. Martin's Press, 2000).

scene at Boston's Faneuil Hall: This story was popularized by Harriet Beecher Stowe, who was not there when it happened but wrote the most famous contemporary portrayal of Truth for *The Atlantic Monthly* and placed it in her native New England. Decades later, Douglass confirmed the story from his own perspective without reference to time or location. While the story is true, its details are somewhat unclear, though historians now place it in Ohio after the Fugitive Slave Act of 1850. See Nell Irvin Painter, *Sojourner Truth: A Life, A Symbol* (New York: Norton, 1996), 160-62.

110 *God was real*: See W. E. B. DuBois, *Black Reconstruction in America: 1860–1880*, introduction by David Levering Lewis (1962; repr., New York: Free Press, 1998), 124.

110 *over a way that with tears has been watered*: James Weldon Johnson was a
poet of the Harlem Renaissance and a central staff person in the early
days of the NAACP. His "Negro National Anthem," from which these
lines are quoted, is sung at Emancipation Day and Black History Month
celebrations throughout the African American community. The patri-
otism it ritualizes, no matter the shade of your skin, is much closer to the
vision of Jesus than the "Star Spangled Banner" or the "Pledge of Allegiance." Communities committed to the Christianity of Christ in America
should teach children to sing this song whenever they stand to remember
their native land. See James Weldon Johnson, "Lift Every Voice and Sing,"
in *The African American Heritage Hymnal* (Chicago: GIA, 2001), 627.
Where Episcopalians have the Book of Common Prayer as a companion
to their Scriptures, African Americans have a hymnbook. Hymns from
the *African American Heritage Hymnal* can be accessed online via
hymnary.org; see, for example, "Lift Every Voice and Sing," http://
hymnary.org/text/lift_every_voice_and_sing.

111 *there is a river*: The Scripture reference is to Revelation 22:1, which
echoes Psalm 46. *There Is a River: The Black Struggle for Freedom in
America* (Orlando, FL: Harcourt Brace, 1981) is Vincent Harding's
monumental history of the black-led freedom movement, which
chronicles the struggle of resistance from the shores of Africa up to
the end of the Civil War. Though he never completed his intended
second volume of this history, Dr. Harding was instrumental in
founding both the King Center, dedicated to continuing the work of
Dr. Martin Luther King Jr., and the Institute of the Black World
(IBW), a research, policy, and advocacy organization now based in
New York City. These institutions, as well as Dr. Harding's many
books and articles, offer a rich resource for anyone who wants to join
the river of resistance in America. See, from the PBS documentary
series American Experience, *Eyes on the Prize: America's Civil Rights
Movement 1954–1985*, a Blackside production for which Dr. Harding
served as an historical adviser. His book *Hope and History: Why We
Must Share the Story of the Movement* (Maryknoll, NY: Orbis, 2010)
is an accompanying resource for groups to reflect on how these
American stories shape faith and action.

112 *21st Century Freedom Ride*: 21st Century Freedom Ride has since become
a regular formation program of the School for Conversion, which has
partnered with the United Methodist Church, the Fund for Theological
Exploration, and several other schools and nonprofit organizations to

offer this experience of a mobile course in freedom-movement history. Learn more at www.schoolforconversion.org/community-education/.

112　*Go from your country*: See Genesis 12. Pilgrimage is a rich Christian tradition that invites people to go deeper into the faith journeys of particular people and places. It was an ancient practice that has been largely neglected by American Christianity. To learn more about pilgrimage in the Christian tradition, see Charles Foster, *The Sacred Journey*, Ancient Practices (Nashville: Nelson, 2010).

Ella's Song: See "Ella's Song," lyrics and music by Bernice Johnson Reagon, recorded by Sweet Honey in the Rock on their album *We All . . . Everyone of Us*, Genius Media, 1983.

114　*Rev. Barber*: I have told a longer version of the story of my encounter with Rev. Barber in Jonathan Wilson-Hartgrove, *Free to Be Bound: Church Beyond the Color Line* (Colorado Springs: NavPress, 2008), 27-40. His own story, which informs much of the analysis in the second half of this book, is told in Rev. Dr. William J. Barber II with Jonathan Wilson-Hartgrove, *The Third Reconstruction: Moral Mondays, Fusion Politics, and the Rise of a New Justice Movement* (Boston: Beacon Press, 2016). Those interested in learning more about Rev. Barber's work to build a moral movement for Reconstruction in America today should visit www.breachrepairers.org and learn more about the Poor People's Campaign: A National Call for Moral Revival. Rev. Barber and I cohost a monthly program called the Gathering, which is livestreamed on the first Sunday of each month and available as a podcast on iTunes and Stitcher.

116　*people such as Clarence Jordan, Will Campbell, and Anne Braden*: For an introduction to some of the white people who have been deeply involved in the black-led freedom struggle, see Drick Boyd, *White Allies in the Struggle for Racial Justice* (Maryknoll, NY: Orbis, 2015). See also the note on William Lloyd Garrison earlier in this chapter.

117　*Get those goddamned n------!*: Sheriff Clark is quoted in Robert A. Pratt, *Selma's Bloody Sunday: Protest, Voting Rights, and the Struggle for Racial Equality* (Baltimore: Johns Hopkins University Press, 2017), 47.

Nicodemus came to visit Jesus: See John 3:1-21.

119　*Nicodemus shows up*: See John 19:38-42.

8 Moral Revival

122　*like the Scriptures say, a ladder*: See story of Jacob's ladder, Genesis 28:10-17.

Every round goes higher: "Jacob's Ladder," African American spiritual.

123   *Dr. King*: Taylor Branch's trilogy on America in the King years offers a detailed chronicle of both Dr. King's public life and the historical characters with which he interacted. See Taylor Branch, *Parting the Waters: America in the King Years 1954–63* (New York: Simon & Schuster, 1988), *Pillar of Fire: America in the King Years 1963–65* (New York: Simon & Schuster, 1998), and *At Canaan's Edge: America in the King Years 1965–68* (New York: Simon & Schuster, 2006). Key historical points in this telling are taken from an older, single-volume biography by Stephen B. Oates, *Let the Trumpet Sound: A Life of Martin Luther King, Jr.* (New York: HarperCollins, 1994). While it takes liberties with history, Ava DuVernay's movie *Selma* is a contemporary resource to introduce people to Dr. King's role in the civil rights movement.

     the story of Lazarus: See Luke 16:19-31.

125   *fusion politics*: This particular form of organizing, developed during Moral Mondays, is taught in the Moral Political Organizing Leadership Institute and Summit (MPOLIS), a workshop offered by Repairers of the Breach (breachrepairers.org). Since 2015, thousands of faith leaders and activists across the United States have been trained in this model, including local and national leadership of the Fight for 15, Movement for Black Lives, Women's March, Democracy Spring, Faith in Public Action, the Samuel DeWitt Proctor Conference, and others. While #MoralResistance and Moral Monday serve as labels to connect these grassroots coalitions, they are locally led and mobilized. Fusion coalitions are not membership organizations but networks of organizations committed to a wide range of issues and committed to working together for the common good according to shared organizing principles. See Rev. Dr. William J. Barber II with Jonathan Wilson-Hartgrove, "Fourteen Steps Forward Together for America's Third Reconstruction," *Beacon Broadside*, January 12, 2016, www.beacon broadside.com/broadside/2016/01/fourteen-steps-forward-together -for-americas-third-reconstruction.html.

126   *Third Reconstruction*: See Rev. Dr. William J. Barber II with Jonathan Wilson-Hartgrove, *The Third Reconstruction: Moral Mondays, Fusion Politics, and the Rise of a New Justice Movement* (Boston: Beacon Press, 2016) for an understanding of Third Reconstruction and also Moral Mondays, which are discussed more fully later in the chapter.

129   *surgical precision*: Diana Gribbon Motz, US Circuit Judge, writing on behalf of the 4th Circuit Court of Appeals in its decision to overturn

the ruling of a lower court in N.C. NAACP v. McCrory. This decision was upheld by the US Supreme Court on May 15, 2017.

131 *Moral Mondays had turned the tide*: See Tom Jensen, "Why Pat McCrory Lost and What It Means in Trump's America," *Portside*, December 8, 2016, www.portside.org/2016-12-10/why-pat-mccrory-lost-and-what -it-means-for-trumps-america.

132 *inspirer of all the reform movements*: Bishop Alexander Walters, *My Life and Work* (New York: Revell, 1917), 241, www.docsouth.unc.edu /neh/walters/walters.html.

9 Having Church

137 *Graham suggested that God*: See Lindsey Bever, "Franklin Graham: The Media Didn't Understand the 'God-factor' in Trump's Win," *Washington Post*, November 10, 2016, www.washingtonpost.com /news/acts-of-faith/wp/2016/11/10/franklin-graham-the-media-didnt -understand-the-god-factor/?utm_term=.48b5ab080488.

speech to the 2016 Democratic National Convention: A video of this speech is available, along with other public speeches and press conferences for Rev. Barber, at the Repairers of the Breach YouTube channel. See, e.g., Rev. Dr. William J. Barber II, "We Must Fight for the Heart of Our Democracy!," July 28, 2016, www.youtube.com/watch?v =DNcP82-trrA.

140 *Greenleaf Christian Church*: Greenleaf is located at 2110 N. William Street in Goldsboro, North Carolina. The church's website offers information about service times (greenleafchristiandoc.org). Services are livestreamed the first Sunday of each month by Fusion Films. Rebuilding Broken Places Community Development Corporation (CDC) is incorporated independently of the church and located across William Street from the church building (see rbpcdc.org).

145 *gospel of the enslaved church is preserved in its songs*: See Albert J. Raboteau, *Slave Religion: The "Invisible Institution" in the Antebellum South*, updated ed. (New York: Oxford University Press, 2004).

145 *I Will Trust in the Lord*: See *The African American Heritage Hymnal* (Chicago: GIA, 2001). One version of this hymn is available at http:// hymnary.org/text/i_will_trust_in_the_lord_i_will_trust_in.

150 *You've become a living member*: For those interested in learning and implementing gospel practices in your congregation and community, the most important step is to establish a mentoring relationship with

the leadership of congregations that have been formed by gospel practices. You can do this in your community. Get to know poor people and ask them which churches are actually good news to them. Visit those churches and see what's going on. In my experience, people doing this work are glad to pass on what they have learned. Two resources that help connect churches in the black-led freedom movement are named after Samuel DeWitt Proctor, a great teacher, pastor, and justice advocate: the Samuel DeWitt Proctor Conference (sdpconference.info) and the Samuel DeWitt Proctor Institute, hosted each summer by the Children's Defense Fund at Haley Farm, outside of Clinton, Tennessee (see childrensdefense.org/programs/faithbased/faith-based-action-programs-pages/Samuel-DeWitt-Proctor-Institute.html). In the evangelical subculture, the strongest black-led movement is the Christian Community Development Association, founded by Dr. John Perkins. CCDA (ccda.org) hosts an annual gathering and also connects churches and ministries committed to gospel practice regionally.

In Mark's Gospel: See Mark 10:17-27.

151 *Brown v. Board of Education*: Brown v. Board of Education, 347 U.S. 483 (1954). This Supreme Court case overturned Plessy v. Ferguson (1896), which had allowed state-supported segregation of schools.

10 Healing the Heart

158 *white fragility*: See Robin DiAngelo, "White Fragility," *International Journal of Critical Pedagogy* 3, no. 3 (2011): 54-70. While I am acknowledging a real source of pain for people who have imagined themselves to be white, DiAngelo is absolutely correct that people who are blinded by whiteness use power to avoid this pain and silence others. This critical work is deeply important for anyone committed to unlearning whiteness as a habit of being in the world.

James Baldwin: The son of a preacher in Harlem, Baldwin became one of the best American writers of the twentieth century—and one of our most insightful critics. His quote here is from an essay first published in *Essence* magazine (April, 1984), "On Being White . . . and Other Lies." A recent documentary offers a powerful introduction to Baldwin's life and work: *I Am Not Your Negro* (Magnolia Pictures, 2017). Baldwin's classic collection of essays on race in America, written during the throes of the civil rights movement, is also essential reading for those committed to racial healing: James Baldwin, *The Fire Next Time* (New York: Dial Press, 1963).

159 *Bob Zellner*: See Bob Zellner with Constance Curry, *The Wrong Side of Murder Creek: A White Southerner in the Freedom Movement* (Montgomery: NewSouth Books, 2008).

161 *trauma science*: Kathryn House, a scholar at Boston University, has taught me about the concept of epigenetics and evidence of fear as an inherited trait in Holocaust studies. While Bob Zellner's notion of the shriveled-heart syndrome is based more on his experience and observation than science, it does seem there is an increasing amount of data to support his thesis.

163 *New monasticism*: See Jonathan Wilson-Hartgrove, *New Monasticism: What It Has to Say to Today's Church* (Grand Rapids: Baker Books, 2010).

Saint Benedict: The two primary sources for Benedict of Nursia are his *Rule of Life*, which he wrote close to the end of his life, and the *Life of Benedict*, which was written by Pope Saint Gregory the Great, who popularized Benedict's life and witness from his position of ecclesial leadership in Rome (see Gregory the Great, *Life of St. Benedict*, commentary by Adalbert de Vogüé, trans. Hilary Costello and Eoin de Bhaldraithe [Petersham, MA: St. Bede's, 1993]). Several years ago I recorded a video introduction to Benedict's wisdom, which you can get on DVD from Paraclete Press. See Jonathan Wilson-Hartgrove, *The Rule of Saint Benedict: An Introduction* (Peabody, MA: Paraclete Video, 2012), DVD. For more on Benedictine spirituality today, see the writing of Kathleen Norris and Sister Joan Chittister.

164 *a book on what white evangelicals can learn from the black church*: See Jonathan Wilson-Hartgrove, *Free to Be Bound: Church Beyond the Color Line* (Colorado Springs: NavPress, 2008).

Epilogue

172 *All have sinned*: Romans 3:23.

ABOUT THE AUTHOR

Jonathan Wilson-Hartgrove is a celebrated spiritual writer and sought-after speaker. A native of North Carolina, he is a graduate of Eastern University and Duke Divinity School.

Jonathan lives with his family at the Rutba House, a Christian community and house of hospitality, in Durham, North Carolina, where he directs School for Conversion (schoolfor conversion.org).

You can learn more about Jonathan's writing at jonathanwilsonhartgrove.com.
You can also follow him on Twitter: @wilsonhartgrove and Facebook: @jonathan.wilsonhartgrove.

ALSO BY
JONATHAN WILSON-HARTGROVE

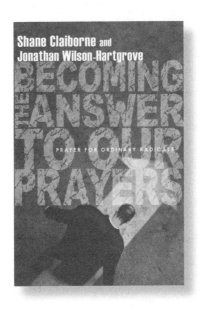